The Hand of God

The Hand of God

A Message of Faith and Love

Catherine Walters

Published by Arbor Books, Inc.

The Hand of God: A Message of Faith and Love
Copyright © 2009 by Catherine Walters
Published by Arbor Books, Inc.

All rights reserved. No part of this book may be reproduced (except for inclusion in reviews), disseminated or utilized in any form or by any means, electronic or mechanical, including photocopying, recording, or in any information storage and retrieval system, or the Internet/World Wide Web without written permission from the author or publisher.

Scripture taken from the HOLY BIBLE, NEW INTERNATIONAL VERSION®. Copyright © 1973, 1978, 1984 International Bible Society. Used by permission of Zondervan. All rights reserved.

The "NIV" and "New International Version" trademarks are registered in the United States Patent and Trademark Office by International Bible Society. Use of either trademark requires the permission of International Bible Society.

Printed in the United States of America

Book design by Arbor Books
www.arborbooks.com

The Hand of God: A Message of Faith and Love
Catherine Walters

1. Title   2. Author   3. Inspirational/Memoir

Library of Congress Control Number: 2009903345

ISBN-10: 0-9818658-6-0
ISBN-13: 978-0-9818658-6-7

Dedicated to the loving memory of my husband Johnny, my best friend, my soul mate, my confidant and who was the best thing that ever happened to me. I will always love you.

FOREWORD

It is easy to imagine God's hands shaping the rolling hills of Fredericksburg, Virginia. It is easy to picture Him carving the Rappahannock River through this landscape to sustain life. To envision Him dotting the hills with an array of yellow poplar, northern red and white oak, pignut hickory, red maple, and Virginia pine to provide a canopy of protection for all living things that seek shelter here. It is easy to see the hand of God at work in a place such as this—a place where, no matter where you cast your eyes, you are overwhelmed by the beauty of life.

But God is not only found in the moments in which we witness great beauty. And faith is what gives us the belief that even in the darkest, bleakest moments, even as we cast our eyes inward in the face of death, we can still see God holding His hand out toward us.

My husband, Johnny Walters, died on June 16, 2007, after a long and brave battle with brain cancer. More courageous than his battle against the disease was his desire to impress upon others the importance of the faith he came to find such great comfort in during the final year and a half of his life. During times of trouble, pain and adversity, God was always there, providing Johnny with His love and grace through the miracle of faith and the unwavering support of family, friends and strangers.

It was Johnny's deep desire to have the opportunity to provide to others the same reassurance God granted him through faith. In telling his story I hope to give him the chance to pass that message on.

This book is Johnny's gift to you and my gift to the man who was the miracle God gave to me.

—Catherine (Cathy) Walters

Though he stumble, he will not fall, for the LORD upholds him with his hand.

Psalm 37:24
New International Version

INTRODUCTION

Towards the end of March 2006, winter in Virginia had come to an end. The weather had turned warm and wet and the trees along the river were bursting with life. For Johnny and Cathy Walters, daily life had taken on its own natural cycle. Rising early every morning, Cathy would shower, change and get herself ready for work. Soon she would make her way downstairs to the kitchen to prepare breakfast.

The kitchen of the Walters' brick, colonial home is one of cherry wood cabinets and Corian countertops. It is a place where the smells of homemade bread and slow-cooked meals hang in the air and warm the soul. Although it was only Cathy and Johnny living at home then, the typical morning in the Walters' kitchen was still a bustle of activity. On any given day fresh-ground coffee beans were percolating with hot water in the coffee maker, bacon was sizzling in a pan, and biscuits were rising in the oven.

Breakfast was eaten in the dining room, in front of a picture window that looked out on the lush, backyard lawn, and the relaxing start to the morning was almost always peppered with conversation, laughter and stretches of comfortable silence. It was during this time, as they sat together, that Cathy would take a few moments to review with Johnny what things he might do during the day while she was off at work at the Dahlgren naval base.

It had been a little over a year before that doctors had discovered two tumors lodged in Johnny's brain. One had been deep inside, the other close to the surface. Over the course of the past year Johnny had already made his way through two brain surgeries and radiation treatments. Of these brain surgeries, the first, to remove the accessible tumor, had resulted in a burst blood vessel that had near-tragic results. Against all odds the second surgery had been a success, and anyone who caught a glimpse of the man eating a quiet breakfast with his wife would never have guessed the hurdles the past year had brought.

However, one of the side effects of this burst blood vessel was the disintegration of his short-term memory. Although day-to-day life was something Cathy and Johnny celebrated in light of his health concerns, the short-term memory loss could be troublesome.

Every morning, as Cathy moved around the kitchen, preparing breakfast, she also gathered and doled out the doses of medicine Johnny was required to take throughout the day. The dose at breakfast was easy for her to monitor and it was always waiting for him when he came downstairs. The doses for throughout the day were a little trickier, and so Cathy came up with her own system. Placing the midmorning and lunchtime pills into separate plastic bags, she would hide them in different areas of the kitchen. Then, at the appointed time she could call home, direct him to the correct bag, and have him take the medicine as she directed him over the phone.

Johnny's short-term memory loss also made it very complicated to ensure that he would eat enough during the day and was why Cathy always made sure that he had a hearty breakfast, and why there was always a pre-made lunch waiting for him in the refrigerator. It was also why it had become habit for her to gently remind him that, amongst other things, she did not want him going down the steep basement steps to his woodworking shop while he was home alone.

A woodworking enthusiast, Johnny had spent years gathering a collection of state-of-the-art tools that he kept in his special area of their basement. He had put these tools to good use on the many projects that had helped him turn their house into a home. As with everything he did, he was meticulous with his hobby. For Johnny, learning to build had not meant simply hunkering down and learning by trial and error how to build something useful. It had meant seeking out the finest craftsmen and picking their minds to learn every aspect of technique, skill and philosophy. It had meant putting in the time to make something as beautiful as it was useful. The house and property were dotted with tables, chairs, benches, birdhouses and other pieces of furniture he had made himself. Many of these pieces were beautifully done in the rustic, sturdy and simple mission style—a skillful reflection of the man who had crafted them.

Once Cathy left for work, Johnny typically took his time finishing his own breakfast and reading the newspaper. The quiet pace of life at home was not something he had adapted to easily. When he had retired from his work as an engineer at Dahlgren naval base, he had left as head of the Weapons Systems Department. Actively serving on various corporate boards, he had been well-known and highly regarded as a strong leader, dedicated as much to the service of his country as to his own team of employees.

Johnny had spent over thirty years working in a civilian capacity for the military and his achievements had been capped by such prestigious awards as the Navy Meritorious Civilian Service Award and the John Adolphus Dahlgren Award. He was used to moving at a fast clip and responding to a constant stream of requests throughout the work day.

Now, to fill his days, he focused on his hobbies of woodworking and photography. On typical mornings he might read and listen to music, and most of all he enjoyed walking, even when it was just a simple stroll to the end of the winding driveway to retrieve the mail.

On an afternoon in late March, the phone rang in Cathy's office at the base, and she answered it. It had been a particularly uneventful day and she was not surprised to hear Johnny's voice on the other end of the line. His greeting could have been the start of any one of the dozen telephone conversations she knew they would share over the course of her eight-hour workday. It was as normal as any other call they had shared—until she asked him a question.

"Is everything alright?"

"Yes," he answered.

"You didn't go down into the basement, did you?" Cathy asked in the concerned way only a woman married to a man for twenty years could—gently asking, cautioning and scolding at the same time.

"I did," he replied.

Perhaps it was something in the tone of his voice that made her question him further. A slight tinge of wonder and disbelief that wasn't generally evident in his naturally calm, Mississippi drawl.

"Johnny—are you alright? You didn't fall?" she asked.

"I did."

After a sharp intake of breath she quickly sought assurance and asked him once again, "Are you sure you're alright?"

"I'm fine," he replied. "But I want you to listen and be quiet until I tell you what happened."

Johnny Walters stood an inch over six feet tall. He was built lean and strong with a warm smile and kind, hazel eyes. At fifty-eight years of age his frame still had a quiet strength that belied the cancerous battle raging inside his body.

The fourteen steps leading down to the basement workshop were steep. As Johnny descended them that morning he suddenly found himself falling. Unable to stop his body from tumbling he soon became turned around and moved through the air backwards. Maybe it was because his hands sought something to grasp onto; maybe it was because he instinctively moved in a way that would break his fall; but Johnny soon found himself turned around, looking at the empty darkness of the space through the back of the open stairs.

As Cathy listened to her husband tell her of his fall, she could picture it happening. An overwhelming feeling of helplessness shot through her.

"And then there was a hand on my back," Cathy heard him say through the phone.

"A hand?"

"A large hand, and it stopped me from falling and pushed me upwards until I was standing steady again," he replied.

Cathy sat at work, listening to her husband describe the afternoon events, and the hair on her arm stood up, and she began to cry. Later, when she arrived home from work, she asked him to tell her the story once again. As he did, Johnny placed his own hand on her back to show her what he had felt that morning. The anxiety over the tragedy that could have occurred overwhelmed her until she felt the strength of Johnny's palm holding her steady.

"Only this hand was bigger and stronger," he told her.

"Whose hand?" Cathy asked him.

"God's" Johnny answered.

Children, obey your parents in the Lord, for this is right. "Honor your father and mother"—which is the first commandment with a promise—"that it may go well with you and that you may enjoy long life on the earth." Fathers, do not exasperate your children; instead, bring them up in the training and instruction of the Lord.

—Ephesians, chapter 6:1-4,
New International Version

CHAPTER ONE

When the Second World War came to an end and the United States Army Air Corps honorably discharged Harding Walters from his services he returned to Scott County, Mississippi. It wasn't long after that when Harding and his wife, Evelyn, welcomed their first son, Tommy Lane Walters, into the world.

Both Harding and Evelyn had been born in the rural Mississippi farm country and raised during the Depression, in near poverty on small farms. They had attended school together and both hoped to provide a more stable way of life for their new son and his future siblings.

During his enlistment Harding had earned extra money cutting the hair of other soldiers. With this in mind, the young couple moved to Brandon, Mississippi, a small town east of Jackson in the very heart of the Magnolia State. Harding was soon enrolled in the barber school at Hinds Junior College, but life for the Walters was a daily struggle. Becoming a barber required an initial year of school and then a second year as an intern, working for the barber who owned the only shop in the small town of 2,500 people.

After his internship with the barber ended Harding made the decision to open his own shop. While he struggled to establish a clientele of his own, the family lived in the cramped quarters of a three-story boarding house.

It was on October 2, 1948 that my husband Johnny Wayne Walters was born. And as we learn through scripture, the Lord does provide. Soon after Johnny was brought home from the hospital the family was able to leave the boarding house behind and settle into a small, post-war house on College Street, a mile out of downtown Brandon. Four years later Harding and Evelyn welcomed their third child to the family. Tommy and Johnny found themselves with a younger sister, Teresa Carol Walters, and their circle was complete.

Brandon, Mississippi, had one red light and a drug store with a soda fountain. For three young children with a sense of adventure, life was filled with the wonderful monotony of exploration and discovery of the world around them. The Walters' house was a mile from downtown, and it sat on a narrow lot of approximately five acres of property. When they first moved in, Harding invested in a cow and would go out early in the morning and supply the family with their morning milk. In either direction, at the front or the back of the small house, the children could wander into the woods and seek out any kind of adventure at all.

Johnny and Tommy, being only three years apart, spent most of their time after school and during the summer joined at the hip, exploring the world around them. On occasion they allowed their sister to join them. From a young age both boys knew the wooded area around their home better than they knew their own home. They navigated their own trails, could tell you where the bee hives were, and knew in an instant what lived in almost any hole in any tree.

But most afternoons they could be found roaming the woods in the front and the back of their home. Long walks, imaginative games of adventure and conversations about life and sports filled hours at a time.

And as it was for many young boys, when they grew old enough, their most treasured possessions were their BB guns.

Whereas roaming the woods had always been fun and enjoyable, now armed with their BB guns, Tommy and Johnny had a purpose. Cans and bottles were scavenged for target practice, and snakes and birds were easily picked off. Soon the boys could stealthily move from tree to tree and shoot with the aim of expert marksmen.

By their early teens the BB guns had become shotguns, and as soon as squirrel season started in the fall the boys would set out with their dog after school and spend hours hunting together. Squirrels were small and fast, and when hunting season began the trees were still at peak foliage, so it took a sharp eye and a quick, steady hand to catch one. They were critters that darted and maneuvered quickly, and there were plenty of small places underfoot to leap inside at a moment's notice.

But most evenings, by the time Tommy and Johnny returned home, each would be carrying enough food for their mother to cook their favorite meals. Fried squirrel, along with gravy, mashed potatoes and the knowledge that they had provided food for themselves and their family, was very satisfying for the young boys.

Because of Harding's long hours working to establish the barber shop and make ends meet for his family, he was only able to accompany his sons on their hunting excursions a few times a year. But he took these outings seriously—and made time for them whenever he could. The long treks into the woods for a hunt gave him ample time to talk to his boys like the men they were quickly becoming, and to teach them by example how to always be responsible for themselves and for each other. Thanksgiving, Christmas and New Year's Day were the few days during the year that allowed him this time with his boys, which he treasured.

One Thanksgiving morning the three Walters men set out into a hardwood forest fifteen miles east of Brandon. It was a cold, wet November for the Deep South that year and there had been a heavy frost that settled on the ground the night before. The hike into the woods that day was not an easy one. The ground was wet and muddy and, where the puddles weren't too deep, the murky water had turned to slippery ice.

After five miles of difficult walking they came to a stream and Harding crossed it, moving carefully over a fallen log. Johnny was next and midway across the ice-covered tree, he slipped and fell into the water. From where Tommy stood, still on the side of the small river bank, it was a funny sight—his brother's arms windmilling through the air as he tried to catch his balance before pitching forward and splashing into the water. But when, with lightning speed, Harding managed to move back across the log and reach into the water to rescue his son, the two boys realized the seriousness of the situation.

The human body is meant to stay at a temperature of approximately ninety-seven degrees. When plunged into icy cold water for even just a few moments, the body reacts swiftly. As Harding pulled his son out of the water he knew this. He also knew that the cold, soaked clothes that covered his son would keep his temperature low, and that there was little time to waste in getting him dried off and warm.

With a tight grip on Johnny's hand, Harding and his two boys ran three miles until he saw some dry wood and stripped his son's clothes off him. Soon, covered in his father's coat and his brother's dry shirt, Johnny started to recover from the shock of the cold. It was another two miles before they could get back to the car and the heater, and throughout the entire ordeal, never once did Johnny whimper or complain.

It was a stoicism embedded in his personality and a characteristic that would be remarked upon again and again. It was also a learning experience for both boys—and would cement in their relationship the responsibility each felt for the other's health and well-being.

In fact, the responsibilities that all three of the Walters children felt for each other and for their family unit is best illustrated by a family tradition that started when they were still quite young. One evening a week was designated as "family night." An event for sure, it meant that after dinner the television was kept off and the family gathered together to read scripture and then discuss the lesson they had just heard.

In addition to discussing the Bible verses, there was also a certain amount of time given to discussing family grievances or troubles of any kind at all. The rules were simple: As long as they spoke respectfully, if a person in the family felt they had been unfairly treated or misjudged, or even wrongly punished, this was the time for them to speak up and be heard. It instilled in all three children an understanding of the importance of communication, along with the strong characteristic ability to question authority in a respectful manner. And there were many times that this ability would work well to Johnny's advantage in his later years.

When Johnny and his brother weren't in school or spending their days on great adventures in the woods, they were proud members of the Southern Baptist church's Royal Ambassadors. The church was a cornerstone of the Walters' family life and the Royal Ambassadors (or RAs, as they referred to themselves) is a Southern Baptist organization that today is over a hundred years old. It was established as a way to teach young, Southern Baptist boys that they were missionaries of Christ, responsible for going out into the world and sharing the story of Jesus through the word of God as well as through their own actions. For the church, it is a way to encourage young boys to find their unique places in spreading the word of God to others, and the two Walters brothers took their service seriously.

However, for young Johnny and Tommy, it also meant the fun of organized activities through summer camp on the coast. Camp life as a Royal Ambassador entailed learning how to be comfortable and safe in God's great outdoors. For young boys fond of adventure and exploration, learning all about first aid, mapping and using a compass, sheltering and building fires was a form of heaven on earth. In addition to the fun it provided, Johnny and Tommy's royal ambassadorship was another way that religion became embedded not only in their spiritual but their everyday life as well.

However, as life has proven time and time again, there is some validity to the idea that "boys will be boys," and stoicism and moral goodness aside, Johnny was as much a boy as any other.

When two brothers are close in age there sometimes exists a natural competition between them. Johnny and Tommy were no exception to this rule. One afternoon, Tommy, feeling the immortality of youth, bet his younger brother that he could ride around Whitfield Road and return back to their house in less than fifteen minutes. Johnny had a natural inclination for math and physics, and noted that his brother was posing a challenge that was not at all possible. He and Tommy agreed to a bet on the spot and within moments Tommy had taken off on his five-speed bike to prove his younger brother wrong.

Whitfield Road had a downhill slope and in order to win the bet against his brother, Tommy knew that he would have to take that hill at the highest speed he could reach. As he leaned far forward and pedaled with all of his might, the rushing air created a whistle of white noise in his ears. There was a moment when he was certain the bet would be his and he'd have trumped his younger brother and claimed victory for himself. But that was only a passing moment, for as Tommy glanced down at the wheel of his bicycle, he watched as the bolt that held the front brakes to the frame vibrated its way right out of the metal.

Although he was certain he had reached maximum speed, everything soon began to move in slow motion. With nothing to hold it in its place, the brake caliper soon slid into the spokes of the wheel. The wheel jammed instantly when the calipers became lodged in the front forks. With his body and the back wheel still moving through the air, Tommy somersaulted over the handlebars and hit the asphalt on his back. By the time he came to a stop his body was covered in cuts and scrapes and his kneecap bore a wound that would heal into a scar that still showed over forty years later.

Limping back to the house, half dragging and half rolling the traitorous bicycle alongside him, Tommy reached the house a good deal later than the fifteen-minute challenge. As he approached the house Johnny took one look at his brother and nodded his head. "I didn't think it was possible," he said.

Life moved along at a slow and steady clip and Tommy left home to enroll in Mississippi State University as an engineering major. Johnny may not have had his brother around for adventures, but he wasn't lacking for things to do. In his junior year of high school he served as vice president of the student council and in his senior year was elected student council president. He was on the band council and a member of the beta club, the Bible club, the homecoming court and the chorus, and was on the staff of the school paper.

One would think that a teenage boy's grades might suffer in the face of all this activity. However, Johnny graduated with honors. At graduation he was awarded the John Philip Sousa band award and the citizenship award. A look through his high school yearbook reveals him highlighted in the hall of fame pages above a list of his many accomplishments. He cut a dashing figure—a tall, athletic and handsome boy on the cusp of becoming a man.

Even with all of these distinctions, after graduation he chose to stay at home and attend Hinds Junior College with the thought that eventually he might go on to law school. Incredibly bright his entire life, Johnny found school at the junior college to be very easy. Harding and Evelyn worried that their son wasn't being properly motivated and together with Tommy, they convinced him to transfer to Mississippi State along with his brother. It was easy for him to fall into engineering as well and the two brothers who had spent most of their youth in each other's shadows were together once again.

Johnny excelled immediately in engineering. His sharp mind adapted quickly to the change in his academic focus and it wasn't long before he was inducted into Theta Tau, the honorary engineering scholastic fraternity. Johnny made the decision to enter the co-op program offered by the engineering school and spent every other semester working full-time for various employers.

One of the most notable accomplishments Johnny did was become the first Mississippi State University student to work outside the United States. The first summer he was enrolled in the program saw him off to London and a whole new adventure. By the time he graduated in 1971 he was ready to embark on what would become a thirty-two-year civilian career with the Navy.

As water reflects a face, so a man's heart reflects the man.
    —Proverbs 27:19, New International Version

CHAPTER TWO

It was a wink that sealed my fate.
In November 1981, I had only recently started working for the United States Navy, in a civilian job, as an administrative secretary at the Naval Surface Warfare Center in Silver Spring, Maryland, also called the White Oak base. The base and my job were still very new to me and I was meeting so many people and learning so many things that many of my first days there felt as though they were all running together. The position I had accepted was not immediately permanent and so all of my focus was on making a good impression in order to see it turn into full-time employment.

At the time I began working for the Navy, Johnny was overseeing a branch that stretched across two different locations. This required him to spend half of the week in Virginia, at the Dahlgren base, and the other half of the week in Maryland at the White Oak base.

Because we met in a work setting, Johnny and I were fortunate to have the opportunity to build a strong foundation of friendship before we even realized that we had a romantic connection. Working with Johnny was wonderful. He was the sort of supervisor who inspired the level of hard work that he expected of his employees.

Since he worked at both bases, I did not see him every day, but those days that I did see him were always my favorites. It wasn't long before I found myself looking forward to the time he spent on the base, and we soon fell into an easy friendship that made work one of my favorite places to be. The occasional lunches we shared were always filled with conversation and laughter, and it wasn't long before I realized that the soothing drawl of his voice could create a safe haven in even the most chaotic environments.

I began to hope that perhaps there was a chance I might eventually grow to be even more important to him; however I did not want to risk our work relationship or our friendship, so I said nothing and just sought to enjoy our time together. There were moments when I suspected Johnny felt the same way. I remember one sunny afternoon, walking outside on base. The sound of a quiet engine was suddenly beside me as Johnny drove along and rolled down his window. "Hop in. Let's go to Florida," he said.

I laughed and told him that I couldn't. "I don't have my purse."

He shrugged his shoulders and said, "Oh well." He was still chuckling as he slowly drove away.

And then, after a few months came the day when I learned he felt the same way. Johnny was standing in a group of people and although my memory of the names and faces of everyone is a blur, this moment stands out very clearly in my memory.

There was a day when I was sitting at my desk. It was located just outside of Johnny's office and I remember that for some reason a group of people had assembled nearby. I took part in whatever discussion was happening and then the group broke away and I walked back to my desk.

For some reason I glanced into Johnny's office at the same time he looked up and saw me approaching. He smiled.

And then he winked.

It was a quiet, friendly gesture. But the warmth of it felt like a ray of sunshine hitting my skin and somehow sent my heart racing and put me instantly at ease. Soon after that our easy friendship soon fell into the beginnings of what was to be the greatest romance of my life. And it happened with an ease that made it seem as though everything was meant to fall into place.

In retrospect, Johnny and I came to realize that we were both meant to meet. The world is a large and wonderful place and yet, somehow. our lives moved in ways that neither of us could expect would lead us to each other. But our meeting was never by accident.

Immediately before accepting the position with Dahlgren I had been considering another place of work. Incredibly, I later came to find out that Johnny had also been offered a position there and had declined it. The way our paths seemed destined to intersect at some point was one of the ways that Johnny and I believed, from very early on, that we were meant to be together. Even more than just finding each other in this vast world, we were fated, as soul mates, to become a part of each other's lives.

Every day I learned of the many things that made Johnny such a special person. He was quick to laugh and had a story for all occasions. He was lighthearted and sincere, jovial and good-humored, and yet also quietly dignified. And it was this strength of character that sent me tumbling headfirst into love.

Watching Johnny lead a team of 165 employees as head of the branch also gave me a real understanding of how others perceived him. Every day I was able to see how his hard work, compassion, integrity and sensitivity inspired those who worked for him. It seemed as though the entire world agreed with what I thought about this wonderful, sensitive soul, for Johnny was extraordinary in all aspects of his life.

His career with the United States Navy began in 1971 when he was twenty-three years of age, and it would span thirty-two years of service until his retirement in 2003. Johnny was recruited by the Navy directly from college, to work as a civilian. His depth of skill in engineering, coupled with his keen communication skills, vaulted him into leadership positions quite rapidly. He rose quickly through the ranks, working his way up within his department until he eventually achieved the position of acting head of the Weapons Systems Department.

As his position elevated and he began to manage larger and larger groups of people, one thing never changed, and that was his commitment to excellence to both to his employer and his employees.

Throughout his career Johnny received many accolades. Some of these included the Dahlgren Award, the Human Awareness Award and the Navy Meritorious Civilian Service Award. In addition to these public acknowledgements of his hard work, he was also often recognized as a positive force behind the scenes of many projects. It was a fairly regular occurrence for assignments to end with Johnny receiving written thanks from those with whom he had worked. One such letter of appreciation praised his ability to provide "the quiet and extremely effective professional leadership needed."

While these various professional recognitions of his hard work were very important to him, it was by far a greater accomplishment in Johnny's eyes whenever he saw evidence that he had earned the respect of his team and his colleagues. For it was their often vocal appreciation of his hard work and dedication as an employer that he treasured most.

When speaking with Steve Collignon, who was one of the people Johnny had been closest with at work, it is evident that the impact Johnny had on those who worked for him was both deeply positive and long-lasting.

Steve gives his own experience of going to work for Johnny as an example of the good-natured employer he could be. Steve had been working for the government for some time when he'd met Johnny. The two of them had hit off an easy friendship as distant colleagues, and would occasionally email or speak with each other. From the very start Steve had known that Johnny was very transparent and extremely honest—one of the few people who really embodied the philosophy of "what you see is what you get."

At the time, Steve hadn't been very happy in his position. He'd been covering the workload for two positions and on occasion would vent about this to Johnny, and about the toll that his three- to four-hour daily commute was taking on his life.

Johnny had been a quick and fair judge of character and already had already known that Steve was the type of person that he wanted to have working for him. It had been a fairly simple equation for Johnny and he'd soon made the proposal for Steve to come and join his team at Dahlgren.

It is one thing to be friends with a person, and another to work for them. At first Steve had hesitated. Leaving a miserable but reliable position for one that was an unknown quantity was going to entail a leap of faith on his part. There was also the matter of the leap of faith that he'd known Johnny was taking on his behalf by offering him the position without ever having worked directly with him before, as well as the fear of possibly jeopardizing a growing and valued friendship.

But, any hesitation had quickly gone away when Johnny had told Steve bluntly, "Look, I know you will do well. But I'll make you this promise. If you find you don't like the job I will help you in any way I can to find the right position. You have my word. And there are no strings attached or hard feelings if you find it just isn't a good fit."

Torn between Johnny's offer and another, Steve had really been won over by Johnny's "no pressure" approach. Additionally, there had been a few other observations Johnny had made that had really hit home with Steve. Johnny's keen ability to discern people had led directly to his sincere desire to help them.

Johnny had known that Steve had some significant personal setbacks as well as the challenges of the job and commute that I already mentioned. But in the discussion, he had commented, "It's time for you to start worrying about yourself. You need to come back to the lab and get better, and I'd like to give you the chance to do that. I understand what you've been through and you'll see—this will end up being a good move for you."

Johnny had been right. Many, many times Steve would remind him how he was indebted to him and in Johnny's way, with a chuckle, he'd say, "Oh, bull!"

As Steve found out, there was little difference between working for Johnny and being his friend. And for the first time in a long time, Steve had found himself doubly rewarded—working in a position he enjoyed for a superior he respected.

Working for Johnny had not only marked a change in Steve's professional life, but in his personal life as well. He clearly remembers Johnny teaching him the importance of keeping a clear balance of work and home. Whenever Steve had been working too hard, or letting a project at work consume his outside hours, Johnny would point out to him, "You're allowing your environment to control your life instead of taking control yourself." It was a lesson that Johnny had taught many people, and like the ripple effect of a pebble tossed into a lake, he'd had a positive impact on many people and their families. And it had come directly from the value that Johnny placed on the person inside each position.

Over time, Steve also rose through the ranks at Dahlgren. At one point, he moved into a position that Johnny was leaving as the two of them simultaneously ascended a level, and Steve became one of a handful of division heads who reported to Johnny. He remembers clearly how Johnny told him quite frankly, as he was leaving the division, that Steve should not to expect any favors because of his past affiliation with the division. Johnny explained that it was important that he be perceived as fair and impartial, especially to the other divisions.

Johnny believed in a level and honest playing field, and although he valued friendships, he preferred an environment built on trust and honesty, not politics or personal biases. Not many people can say those words without making them sound like a challenge or a warning, but coming from Johnny they were a vote of confidence. And it was acknowledgement that no favors would be given because none would be necessary.

What gave Johnny the ability to be so frank with his employees in this manner was the fact that it was widely recognized that Johnny never had a personal agenda behind any action. No matter what he was doing at work, or what he was telling those who worked for him to do, there was never a doubt that the action at hand was for their own good, or for the good of the team.

As a leader, Johnny had strong faith in the members of his team, and it was this ability to see the positive in everyone that allowed him to successfully manage larger and larger numbers of people. It was a part of his nature to place a high value on the people in his life, a lesson learned in the way his parents had raised him and one he was able to draw on in his job. The strength of his own character allowed him to believe in the characters of those around him. And for those lucky enough to have him as a superior, he made certain they knew he believed 100 percent in their skills and abilities.

Johnny's faith in people to inevitably rise to meet the challenges they were faced with was a strong motivator for those in his department. At times it ran like a current of electricity, jolting a person back to reality from whatever ledge of uncertainty they had been looking out at.

Sometimes doubting your own abilities makes it a little easier to fail at a difficult task. But when Johnny believed in you, sometimes in the face of great adversity, that belief alone was enough to give you the confidence to succeed.

Things weren't always perfect, and there were times when all the encouragement in the world couldn't help a person struggling at work. At those times, when all else had failed and no amount of positive coaching and encouragement would solve a problem, Johnny was never prepared to give up on anyone. He believed that if someone did mess up, it was management's job to recover them, not leave them in the ditch. For those who others would refer to as "problem employees," Johnny would often comment that they were just in the wrong jobs.

When faced with an employee who didn't seem to be the right fit for the position they were assigned to, Johnny was quick to focus on their strengths, maneuvering them into a place that would utilize their best abilities and allow them a better chance for success. He knew and valued the worth of the dedicated people who worked for him and held every member of his team in high regard. It was one of his proudest accomplishments to privately recount the number of folks he helped find their way to a rewarding position.

When BRAC (Base Realignment and Closure) forced the Navy to scale back and close bases across the United States, the portion of Johnny's branch that was located in Maryland was amongst those slated to be shut down. When faced with the knowledge of White Oak closing, it affected him greatly.

The very thought of people who had shown dedication and

loyalty to him and the Navy through the years being told they no longer had jobs tore right to the core of Johnny. He spent sleepless nights worrying about how mortgages were going to be paid and groceries bought. He felt an intrinsic responsibility for the people who worked for him. Typically, as it was whenever he was faced with a challenge, action was his reaction. Johnny refused to stand around and wring his hands helplessly, using the budget cuts as an excuse for putting family finances in jeopardy.

He worked tirelessly, leaving no stone unturned and even in the face of such a daunting task, never once considered accepting defeat. In the end, his perseverance paid off and everyone affected by the realignment who did not want to retire had a job.

For Johnny, there was nothing particularly heroic about this accomplishment. It was simply what any good manager would do for his team, and more importantly what any good person should do for another.

Others who reflect on their experiences with Johnny are always quick to acknowledge his dedication to his team as well as his deft communication skills. Those Thursday evenings back in Mississippi, when the television had been turned off and the family had gathered in the living room to read different stories from the Bible and then take time to communicate with each other, had gone a long way to forming the strong foundation of Johnny's management skills.

From a young age, Johnny had seen first-hand the quick, positive results that a person could get from discussing problems immediately with a person, and working together towards a fair and even solution. It allowed him, as an adult, to be confident in his ability to approach adversity in a pragmatic and practical way, leaving personal emotions out of the equation and understanding the cooperation necessary to reach an amenable resolution.

Additionally, even faced with the most adverse situations, he had an instinctual ability to defuse any disagreement by talking it through rationally and never raising his voice.

When it came to Johnny's professional life he believed in the importance of maintaining a work/life balance. He recognized that one of the best ways to have the energy and the drive to focus completely at work was to give the same dedication and focus to his private life. He actively encouraged his employees to make this same philosophy into a practice.

Johnny was an excellent boss, but his expectations of those who worked for him were high, and often meeting those expectations was a demanding job. Knowing the hard work they put in during the day, when occasionally an employee would let Johnny know that they were leaving early to attend a school event, or get home a little early to enjoy time with their family on a hot summer afternoon, he was known to nod his head, smile, and say, "Don't let the door hit you on the way out."

Typically early to arrive on base in the mornings, he would often push through extremely busy days, dotted with many meetings and great quantities of paperwork. While Johnny enjoyed his job immensely his hard work throughout the day was really always driven by the knowledge that when he reached the end of the day, he would be leaving to go home to his family and a life completely separate from the hectic one on base that fueled his strong drive.

Johnny retired from the Navy in 2003. When he left he was the acting head of the Weapons Systems Department and we threw him a big party. It was a joyous occasion filled with friends and family and coworkers who toasted his career and retold stories about life at the office with Johnny. Recollections of his favorite tie to wear for important meetings (covered in Mickey Mouse faces). Or his flair for dispensing humor during long, tedious meetings.

Steve recalled one specific time when he'd followed Johnny to a board of directors meeting. Johnny had been acting department head at the time. The technical director had gone through a particular aspect of the new pay system and wanted opinions. There had been silence, and then finally Johnny had opened the floor with, "I think it sucks."

The technical director had been the kind of leader that liked openness and after the laughing had stopped, gave Johnny the floor. Johnny had carefully explained his view and when he'd finished, had many others, who had originally been quiet, voicing agreement. Johnny had been confident in his views and had a way of keeping the spirit light, yet he packed real substance behind his thoughts.

The retirement party itself was such a gift to him, to mark the end of many hard years with the people who had made it all worthwhile. Johnny's decision to retire was partly fueled by his strong desire to have a balanced life. It was the next logical step for him after putting in years of service. He was looking forward to the chance to have more time to appreciate the little things in life.

Once retired, he began working as a principal engineer for DTI Associates, a company that consulted with the Navy. The opportunity was one he had worked hard for, and he saw it as the perfect way to continue in a job he loved with many of the same people whose company he so enjoyed, and yet have the chance for us to spend more time together.

Be very careful, then, how you live—not as unwise but as wise, making the most of every opportunity, because the days are evil. Therefore do not be foolish, but understand what the Lord's will is.
　—Ephesians 5:15-17, New International Version

CHAPTER THREE

Johnny and I married in June 1986 in a very small ceremony at our house in Virginia. Soon, his two sons, Ross and Matthew, were spending the weekday evenings with us, which allowed them to attend school in King George.

Johnny loved having the boys around and early in the morning, before he left for the base, he would make their lunches. Chaos reigns supreme in any household where young children have to be out the door in time to make the school bus pickup. Mornings in our home were no different. Faucets running, toilets flushing, and then the pounding of stampeding feet as Ross and Matt raced to grab their jackets and book bags. And without fail, even though their dad was usually already miles away, sitting at his desk, hard at work, two brown lunch bags packed with sandwiches, juice and snacks would be waiting next to the stove.

Ross remembers those rare occasions when he or Matt would race out, forgetting to grab the lunches. Returning to the house in the evening, they would inevitably be faced with a stern-faced father and a lecture. Without ever raising his voice, Johnny would sternly explain to them the importance of showing respect and valuing those things that other people took time to do for you.

Weekends were filled with all sorts of sports and lessons. For a while, when he was in high school, Ross took guitar lessons on Saturday mornings, and Johnny would drive him to his lesson and then wait to drive him home. Johnny was happy that his son had taken an interest in music and he was always eager to see what he learned over the years of Saturday lessons.

When Ross was in the eleventh grade, Johnny decided to go and watch him perform in a school talent show. Ross subtly tried to dissuade his dad from going, but Johnny insisted that he was eager to be there, to continue to actively participate in Ross' musical pursuits. It puts a smile on Ross's face even now when he thinks of his father sitting somewhere in the audience, watching attentively as Ross broke out in a long and loud rendition of Led Zeppelin's "Stairway to Heaven." After the show Johnny told Ross that he thought he had performed well, but Ross remembers with a chuckle that Johnny didn't make the trip back the following year, when his band elected to play "Sunshine of Your Love" by Cream.

On those rare occasions when we weren't overscheduled with music, sports or running errands, Johnny enjoyed taking the boys to the many parks and playgrounds that dotted the Virginia landscape. Memories of running through the woods with his brother, Tommy, for hours on end in Mississippi were some of Johnny's fondest. It was very important to him that Ross and Matt feel the same exhilaration of exploring new places and developing a love for the great outdoors.

One of the places Johnny was fond of taking the boys was Alum Springs Park. There, they could cross the stream that wound through the fields by hopping from stone to stone until their sneakers were soaking wet. The three of them enjoyed exploring rock formations, scaling large rocks and using nature to help them invent all sorts of adventure games.

Another park that Johnny was fond of was Wakefield, the national park that lay approximately forty miles east of Fredericksburg, on the southern shores of the Potomac River, and protected the boyhood home of George Washington. Once there, the four of us could spend hours walking through the sandy shoreline, looking for sharks' teeth.

Johnny thoroughly enjoyed watching the boys race around the great outdoors, and a part of me can't help but think that he loved being there because so many of his own happiest childhood memories came alive during these outings.

Like many people, when I reflect on the things that helped shape my marriage, my mind immediately works to recall momentous occasions like holidays, birthdays, weddings and even funerals. One might assume that these great shifts in life are the ones that define a relationship. However, as time has passed, I have come to find that the memories I most cherish spring from the small moments of joy Johnny and I shared every day.

There are so many instances of happiness in life that pass in the blink of an eye. We know as we are living them that they are the very gifts that make our time on this earth so precious. And yet, during these moments, even as we are appreciating their significance, for the most part they feel as though they are slipping through our fingers like grains of sand. But as cruel as this swift passage of time may be, God in his infinite wisdom has bestowed on us a gift: the power of memory.

And as time passes, the value of these memories grows. Memories are the evidence that we have lived and loved. They are the lessons learned and rewards reaped from chances taken. And they are the very things that we draw strength upon in times of trouble and despair.

My own cherished memories of special times during my marriage to Johnny are, for the most part, these fleeting moments of happiness that were sparked from a look, or a touch, or a kind and loving word.

Johnny and I had many enjoyable moments when the boys were around, but we also had time alone when they were not staying with us, and as they grew up and developed active lives of their own.

On weekends there were many afternoons where there were just the two of us in the house. On Saturdays and Sundays, typically, Johnny would be down in the basement, in his woodworking shop, and I would be rambling around upstairs, doing various chores. Some days, for no apparent reason, he would step away from whatever project he was working on and wander upstairs. Soon, the two of us would be flopped across the bed, talking about anything and everything under the sun.

Weekends also meant the opportunity to cook. Both Johnny and I loved nothing more than an excuse to whip up something delicious in the kitchen. An avid bread baker, he found a great deal of satisfaction in the process involved in baking bread. His favorite recipes to make were sourdough and French bread. There were not many things that could make Johnny smile as broadly as he did on the evenings when we would sit down at the table to enjoy fresh loaves of bread, crab soup and a bottle of wine.

When it was my turn in the kitchen I could always count on the fact that Johnny would find an excuse to stop in, interrupt me, and do something to make me laugh. There were afternoons when he would jump out of nowhere with a devilish glint in his eye and chase me around the room. It never failed to make my heart skip a beat and soon we would be running around the house like two kids, laughing and yelling.

Or, what makes me chuckle even now when I think about it was the time that he ordered, through some catalog, a pair of funny, buck teeth. He strolled into the kitchen and when I looked up to greet him he said, "Hey, babe," and flashed a hideous grin. I was so taken aback that I screamed. And then we laughed until tears were rolling down both of our faces.

Johnny could spend hours in his basement woodshop, and it was there that he made many of the beautiful pieces of furniture that are on display throughout our home. As he was with many things, Johnny was a perfectionist when it came to his woodworking. The diligence, care and patience with which he approached each piece always astonished me—none more so than one of my most cherished gifts from him.

It was Christmastime and Johnny had been working on some woodworking projects that year, but one that I had no idea about was a jewelry box. Throughout that fall and into the early winter I had been on the hunt for a pretty jewelry box in which to store some of my nicer things. It was something I may have mentioned in passing, but I certainly hadn't even realized it had taken root in his consciousness.

That Christmas morning, as I opened my gifts, I was speechless when I opened the present from him. It was quite simply more beautiful than any of the jewelry boxes I had seen in the stores. I am not sure what touched my heart more—the fact that he had thought to make me one, or the effort that he had so obviously put into building it.

I thought about how many hours he had been in the basement, being so careful to make sure that I had no idea what he was working on for my surprise. It was just one of the many ways that Johnny showed me how much he loved me.

Gifts from Johnny were always well thought out and he took so much joy in giving them. For a quiet man, Johnny's capacity to love was immeasurable, and it often spilled out in the form of his thoughtful gifts.

One year, on my birthday, we were supposed to go to California for a short vacation. Johnny had been hit with the flu, and we had decided to cancel the trip and stay home. He was laying in bed, and I knew he felt awful that we were missing our trip. I remember him sitting up and calling me upstairs, and I thought perhaps he needed something to drink or eat. As I approached the bed, he reached out his hand and patted the space next to him, where there was a lump underneath the covers.

"There's something in the bed, babe," he told me. I was confused for a moment and he had me sit down. "Right here." He patted it again, and I reached under the covers, pulling out a small, velvet box.

When I opened it, Johnny watched anxiously as I found inside a beautiful, diamond band. It amazes me now that even stricken with the flu and absolutely miserable, he found it so important to concentrate on making me happy.

Johnny and I loved to travel. It was one of the things he looked forward to doing more of once he retired. We always pictured ourselves exploring more new places as we grew older, and so memories of the trips we took while Johnny was alive are even more precious to me now than they were when we were exploring those new places.

A few years ago we planned a two-week vacation out west. Sitting down at the kitchen table with a map, we planned out our itinerary and made reservations all across the southwest. The trip started out with a flight into Las Vegas. When we walked into the lobby of the hotel, lugging our suitcases, we stopped on the way to the registration desk to play a slot machine. Within minutes Johnny had hit a small jackpot and we checked into our room $150 richer.

After a short time in Vegas we rented a car and began our trip in earnest. We drove to Laughlin, Nevada, and then on to San Diego, California. We passed windmill farms that were so vast, their magnitude took my breath away, and we drove alongside cotton fields that seemed to stretch to the horizon. We visited the Coronado Hotel and Sea World, and then pressed on to Los Angeles. There, we took a bus tour of the stars' homes and waited in line to attend a taping of the *Tonight Show*.

Driving up the coast of California was especially beautiful and I remember stopping to spend a few hours on the beaches of Malibu, swimming in the ocean and sitting on towels in the sand, just taking in the beauty of the ocean and coast around us.

We were awed by the entire state, from the natural beauty of the redwood forests to the manmade beauty of Hearst Castle. But Johnny's favorite time was sitting down at Fisherman's Wharf in San Francisco, enjoying sourdough bread and a bottle of beer and watching all of the different people pass us by.

Our trip was dotted with good food and good times, whether it was dressing up for a nice dinner or stopping to grab a bite to eat at Jack in the Box. One of our favorite stops was in Gilroy, California, the garlic capital of the world, where the air carried the warm, inviting smell of garlic.

Although we saw so many things, and visited so many places, my favorite moments were the hours we spent together in the car. We drove for hours, the radio off and the sound of our voices, talking about everything and nothing, filling the interior of the car.

Every moment was an adventure, and as we took in the sites

at these places and others, Johnny was a wealth of information, informing me of various little facts and stories about every place we visited.

On this and many of the other vacations that Johnny and I took throughout our twenty years of marriage, I knew in the moments, as we were experiencing them, that I would always hold these memories dear to my heart.

I consider that our present sufferings are not worth comparing with the glory that will be revealed in us.
 —Romans 8:18, New International Version

CHAPTER FOUR

In January 2006 both Johnny and I fell ill with the flu. It seemed to be a particularly nasty strain of the illness and our recoveries were slow but steady. About a week after we started feeling better, Johnny began to complain about a buzzing and clicking noise in his ear. Because we'd both had head colds while stricken with the flu, our first thoughts were that it was somehow related to that.

More annoyed than concerned, Johnny made a brief visit to our primary care physician, Dr. Mussey. The doctor checked and found fluid present in his ear. As had been apparent to us, the doctor agreed that Johnny had possibly contracted an inner ear infection while he had the flu, and expected the infection and the annoying noises to subside with the help of some antibiotics.

A month later the buzzing and clicking sounds were still bothering Johnny. Annoyance had grown to mild concern so we drove to Richmond to see an ear, nose and throat specialist that we had both seen as patients before. This specialist confirmed that there was no longer fluid present in Johnny's ears, and the hearing test he performed on Johnny revealed perfect auditory levels. Without clear answers to provide us with, the specialist went ahead and arranged for Johnny to have an MRI at a Richmond hospital.

The appointment was scheduled for early in the morning. There was a snow storm moving north that was expected to hit the area sometime during the night. Knowing how difficult it could be to secure doctor appointments, and not wanting to wait any longer to find out what was wrong, Johnny and I decided to make hotel reservations and spend the night in Richmond. The next morning we went to the hospital, where they performed the MRI and a few days later, the ear, nose and throat specialist called to give us the results.

He explained that the test had not revealed any obvious answers to the problems Johnny had been having. The doctor told him to wait a few weeks and then give him a call back and let him know if the symptoms still persisted.

Still agitated by the noises in his head, Johnny refused to believe that they were a normal occurrence. It had only been a week since our visit to Richmond, but he called the ear, nose and throat doctor and told him that things had not improved. It took some prodding but finally the doctor arranged for Johnny to visit a neurologist. The earliest appointment, we were told, was at the end of March—another long month away.

It wasn't long after this that Johnny began to experience a tingling sensation that would travel down his left arm. The buzzing and clicking noises grew louder, and we were certain that waiting for the neurology appointment in March was no longer a viable or an intelligent option. One of the most frustrating things a person can experience when dealing with a health problem is trying to convince medical professionals that something is wrong, only to have them run tests and reassure you that your health is nothing less than excellent.

Trying to explain his symptoms and express his concerns was beginning to frustrate Johnny, and it isn't hard to imagine how a person might come to the conclusion that the best thing to do is "grin and bear it." Thankfully neither of us was ready to give up pursuing an answer, and we pushed forward.

Watching Johnny's frustration grow was not easy and the only contribution I could think to make was to call Dr. Mussey again. When I explained our plight and Johnny's frustrations he had us in for a visit that afternoon. At his office, when we went through the timeline of symptoms, events and doctor visits that we had been through since we'd last seen him in January, he began to grow concerned. He asked us to get the MRI film and report from the hospital in Richmond.

With a growing sense of urgency Johnny and I drove to Richmond to get the report. Once he had the film Dr. Mussey consulted with a neurologist and then asked us to come and meet with him in his office two days later.

On the day that we were scheduled to meet with Dr. Mussey, I was hopeful. When I looked at Johnny all I could see was a strong, healthy man. After twenty-one years he was still my rock. Although he had partially retired and I knew that as the years passed by, neither of us was getting younger, he was still in excellent shape. He enjoyed long, daily walks that were typically two to three miles in length, he worked countless hours in his basement woodworking shop, and he had spent most of the winter doing strenuous renovations on our house. His health had always been strong and even as he suffered through these symptoms he was far from exhibiting anything that remotely resembled a debilitating or life-threatening disease.

In my mind it was much more likely that there was a simple answer to what he had been experiencing. After all, we had already been to see numerous doctors and Johnny had even undergone as comprehensive a test as an MRI to try to figure out what the problem was. During all of that, nobody had discovered anything dangerously wrong, and so I never expected Dr. Mussey to say anything different now.

Truthfully, I was more worried that we wouldn't be able to find an answer for what was ailing Johnny. Knowing how much the symptoms were bothering him and taking away from the enjoyment of what should have been a relaxing retirement, I hated the thought of his having to deal with inconveniences like the noises in his head or the numbness in his arm.

Dr. Mussey sat down at his desk. "I have bad news for you," he said rather bluntly before softening his voice and looking at Johnny, "You have brain tumors."

There was a brief silence after the doctor delivered this news, and in that moment the air left my lungs in one single rush, and I couldn't seem to draw any oxygen back in. And then, when I finally breathed again, I couldn't stop. It felt like all of the air in the world was forcing itself into my lungs. I was hyperventilating and it felt like I might drown in the air.

In that one instant it felt as though my entire world had been flipped upside down, and then I felt two hands gently pulling on my arm as Jean, Dr. Mussey's nurse, coaxed me out to the waiting room.

I have no idea how long we were out there. It was long enough that my breathing steadied slightly and the uncontrollable crying that had racked my entire body was now a silent stream of tears racing down my cheeks. Johnny stayed in Dr. Mussey's office and when the two men came out into the waiting room, he was still calm. Saying goodbye to the doctor and the nurse that afternoon was a blur. I don't remember much of anything. At some point they instructed us that arrangements had been made for Johnny to meet with the neurologist two days later, and not long after that we left the building and walked to our car.

Inside the car I turned in my seat and looked at him. That was all it took. The drowning sensation flooded my emotions and I had the overwhelming sense that everything that was important to me was being wrenched from my grasp. Brain tumors—how could that be possible?

Johnny and I had been married for twenty-one years. We had worked hard and been contributing members of society. Only minutes earlier I'd still had the luxury of the certainty that we would grow old together. That we would spend the next thirty years of our marriage traveling the world, surrounding ourselves with our friends and family, and spending endless days enjoying each other's company.

All of this was racing through my mind as I sat in the car and watched him. My breath began to choke me again when he turned and looked me squarely in the eyes.

"Cathy, I need you to be strong." His voice was quiet and yet it carried a sense of urgency, an underlying plea that I had never heard before. "You have to be strong for me."

Johnny Walters had been my entire life for so long and that was the first moment he had ever told me that he needed anything from me. It occurred to me that I was being given a chance to prove to him how important he was to me and I suddenly felt completely focused. The crying subsided. I pushed all of the awful thoughts from my mind and told myself that during this storm I would be his shelter. I was determined not to let him down.

Neither of us slept well the next two nights. Johnny lay awake knowing there was a time bomb in his skull and that it would take an enormous reserve of strength and courage to defuse it. And I lay awake next to him knowing fear was a time bomb in my heart that I would have to defuse if I were going to be the reserve of strength and courage that he would need to call on during whatever was ahead.

At 9:45 on Friday morning we arrived at the Neurology Associates of Fredericksburg, located at the base of Mary Washington Hospital. The neurologist that Dr. Mussey had consulted came into the room and took the MRI report from us. We waited quietly for him to return.

"You have something in your head," he explained to Johnny, referring to the brain tumors.

Next he ran a battery of motion tests in the room, having Johnny follow his finger and then do various walking movements across the floor.

"I'm going to put you in the hospital," he said.

After eight weeks of pursuing doctor appointments and waiting for results and answers, the world of medicine had seemed to revolve in slow motion. When the doctor said he was going to put Johnny in the hospital I automatically assumed that meant we would schedule a day for him to go in for more tests. I was wrong, and at that moment I learned how very fast life can change.

We were instructed to go directly up the hill to the registration offices where the hospital had a bed already waiting for Johnny. Once again I climbed into the car feeling as though life was spinning out of my control. Johnny said softly, "I knew this morning that I wouldn't be going home."

Mary Washington Hospital is a 412-bed hospital where patients are given private rooms and wonderful care. Johnny settled into a room and spent the next few days undergoing a battery of tests. We remained fairly optimistic, and some days, when I would walk into the room and see him sitting up, watching television, dressed in his sweats instead of a hospital gown, I felt as though I were visiting him in a hotel rather than a hospital.

It had been explained to us that brain tumors, when cancerous, are usually a secondary form of the disease. The doctors at Mary Washington spent the next few days running blood work and various other tests on Johnny, trying to figure out if there was a primary cancer elsewhere in his body, or if the tumors in his brain were primary. Every test came back normal, and we and the doctors were baffled.

We knew there were two tumors in Johnny's head. One was too deep inside to reach through surgery, and the second was close to the surface. However, the results of the tests were showing him to be completely healthy. The irony of it was that had we not known about the tumors from the MRI, the doctors would have been giving Johnny the good news that it appeared he would live to a ripe, old age.

The neurologist recommended that we speak with the neurosurgeon (Dr. Berlad), so we did. Dr. Berlad told us that the next step was to take out the tumor close to the surface and biopsy it. A biopsy would be able to tell us many things that the other tests had not been able to reveal. By testing the cells of the tumor the doctors would be able to tell exactly what type of cancer we were dealing with as well as where in Johnny's body it had originated.

Because most brain tumors are secondary appearances of cancer, metastasizing from cancer elsewhere in a person's body, the question that we were trying to answer was, where is the cancer originating from? This information would be vital to forming a plan of action to fight the disease, and we were sure that once we had a strategy Johnny would be able to come home and focus on getting better.

Dr. Berlad had likened removing the tumor that sat near Johnny's skull to "picking a cherry out of a bowl of Jell-O." After a few discussions it seemed as though surgery was the simple, straightforward answer. However, Dr. Berlad also explained to us that with any surgery, there were risks. Johnny and I talked about the few options we seemed to have, and although he was nervous we both agreed that the surgery was the right decision.

Prior to any scheduled surgery forms need to be filled out, and the hospital also asked Johnny to address the idea of a living will. The reality of these possible surgical outcomes, written out in black and white on paper, forced us to address possibilities neither of us wanted to think about. As we discussed the surgery and reviewed the risks, Johnny and I talked about the worst things that might happen. One of these possibilities was that he could wind up unable to speak or walk, or worse.

Neither of us wanted to discuss it, but Johnny was an engineer, and in making any decision he was very pragmatic. So even though we were optimistic, he also wanted to discuss the worst possible outcomes. We agreed that if something so terrible as a coma or even worse were to happen, and he could hear me or wanted to signal to me—that squeezing my hand would mean "I love you," "I'm okay," and "I'm fighting."

During the days leading up to his surgery Johnny's sister, Teresa, was on a Beth Moore religious retreat for Bible study with her best friend, Kathy. It was the first time Teresa had attended such an event, and she was eager to spend some time with friends and have some quiet time to focus on her faith. Over the previous weeks Johnny had checked in with her several times to update her on the various doctor visits he'd had. For a while he'd thought that the tingling in his arm and the noises in his ears might be a form of vertigo, which Teresa had suffered from a few years earlier, and he had called her and discussed his symptoms at length with her.

When Dr. Mussey had given us the diagnosis about the brain cancer, Johnny had called Teresa to let her know what was going on. Now that he was undergoing further tests to decide on a treatment, she was anxious to hear about the treatment options and checked in with Johnny numerous times over those days, calling often to find out the results of the various tests the doctors were running on him. A breast cancer survivor herself, Teresa was all too familiar with the toll such an assault has on both the body and the mind. Johnny took great comfort in the knowledge that Teresa had had the strength to beat her cancer, and their conversations helped buoy his spirits as we waited for more information on his disease.

As the weekend progressed, and it became clear to the doctors that Johnny was suffering from primary brain cancer, Teresa joined the other women on the retreat in prayers, and together they prayed for Johnny and our family. She told him repeatedly that she would come up to the hospital as soon as we felt like we needed her, and as soon as we decided he would undergo the surgery, he asked her to fly up.

Teresa stayed with me at the house and the morning of the surgery we arrived at the hospital by 5:45. The nurses prepared Johnny for the operation and as he lay on the gurney I followed along, holding his hand. We took the elevator with them as far as we could and then Teresa and I went to wait.

The waiting room was quiet at first, and then gradually it began to fill up with people who were waiting on their loved ones having surgery.

At about noon Dr. Berlad came out to greet us.

"Everything went really well," he told us. "It couldn't have gone better." I hugged him and cried and he explained to us that Johnny would remain in the intensive care unit (ICU) for twenty-four hours, and then go to a step-down unit before being returned to a regular room for recovery. Then he told me that I could go in and visit.

I wasn't sure what to expect when I saw him. There were still many possible outcomes on the path to full recovery, but by the time I arrived in the ICU he was already beginning to wake up.

"I can't wait to get home and mow the grass," was one of the first things he said when he was alert enough to speak. His recovery in those first twenty-four hours was quick and his spirits were much higher than I'd anticipated. He had made it through the surgery, and while we knew there was still a tumor left in his head, we were confident that the biopsy would tell us what we were dealing with and finally give the doctors a way to outline our plan to fight it.

God gives us adversity in life, but he also gives us a plan to deal with it and we were confident that the information from the biopsy would help us form a plan as well, and we waited to find out what that plan would be.

Because you have so little faith, I tell you the truth, if you have faith as small as a mustard seed you can say to this mountain, "Move from here to there" and it will move. Nothing will be impossible for you.
   —Matthew 17:20, New International Version

CHAPTER FIVE

The incision that they had made in Johnny's skull was much smaller than I had imagined it would be, and when I went into the ICU he had only a little bandage covering it on the side of his head. After twenty-four hours he was moved into the step-down unit, and at that point he was already trying to get up to walk. He moved around the room with help, and that bolstered our optimism.

However, that evening, Teresa and I went to go eat some dinner in the cafeteria and when we returned we both noted a marked change in his personality. For the first time throughout the entire ordeal he was depressed and angry and kept apologizing for being sick. It was as though his mood had taken a 180-degree turn. In retrospect these were all signs that perhaps things were not going as we thought. But even the strongest people sometimes succumb to depression after major surgery and Teresa and I thought that perhaps it was a just small chink in the incredibly strong armor that was Johnny's personality.

Still, his change of mood was unnerving and we stayed late that evening, both of us taking turns trying to cheer him up.

Teresa's faith in God had been one of the strengths she had drawn on through her own battle with cancer and she spent some time that night talking to Johnny about God, and how her belief in His will for her life had gotten her through the times during her illness when she had doubted her own strength.

Lying in a hospital bed, stricken with a devastating illness, is not the easiest time to open your heart and your mind and accept on faith God's will for the plan of your life. Johnny had spent much of his childhood believing strongly that God has a plan for all of us. But as the years progressed, and he became gradually more removed from the roots of his faith, God's will became a harder concept to accept purely on faith. An analytical, pragmatic person, Johnny's world had become a place of facts and figures.

The facts of the medical reality we were dealing with at that moment were grim but the figures we knew about survival gave us hope. In those moments it was easier for Johnny to find hope in the tangible things, like medicine and science, than it was to find hope in the intangible grace of God.

After a while, Teresa left the room and Johnny and I spent some time alone. I tried to cheer him up as well, and at times I believed it was working, only to watch as he grew agitated again. Throughout the evening he would apologize for being sick, for being so much trouble, for not being able to will himself better. I hoped that a good night's sleep would reinvigorate his spirits. Teresa and I left the hospital around ten o'clock that evening and drove the thirty minutes home, both of us worried and tired.

As we drove through the night, and then arrived at home to go to sleep, there was a nurse making the rounds on Johnny's floor. Most of the patients had gone to sleep and Johnny was laying back, resting as well. As the nurse moved about busily, checking his medicine and his vitals, she chatted softly on the phone. Dr. Berlad was at home and she was speaking to him about adjusting Johnny's medicine dosages. Chatting on the phone, she felt Johnny reach out and when she looked at him he said to her in a very calm voice, "Something just popped in my head."

Before she could ask him any questions, Johnny's eyes rolled back in his head and he fell back onto the pillows.

The nurse reacted quickly. She spoke into the phone telling the doctor what had just happened. Listening to her description Dr. Berlad sensed immediately that Johnny had just suffered from a blood vessel bursting in his brain. He was able to direct the nurse to get Johnny immediately to the ICU. He also instructed her to have the medical team give Johnny the medicines necessary to clot whatever blood was surely seeping into his head, and the nurse hung up the phone and leapt into action while Dr. Berlad rushed to the hospital.

I had only been in bed a short time when the telephone rang.

The voice on the other end of the line was crisp and clear, "Mrs. Walters, we need you to come to the hospital immediately, your husband is non-responsive."

I jumped up from the bed and raced around the room, throwing on my clothes. Within minutes I was at Teresa's door at the other end of the house, and I burst into the room. Exhausted as we both were, it appeared that neither of us had been able to ease into sleep that evening. Teresa had heard the phone ring and was standing, almost frozen, waiting.

"Johnny's non-responsive, we have to get to the hospital immediately," I said, and she too gathered her things and got dressed.

"Go start the car, I'll be out in a moment," she instructed.

I ran out to the garage and got into the car. The nurse's words kept repeating in my ear and time seemed to stand still and yet fly past simultaneously.

"Your husband is non-responsive."

Non-responsive. Those were the same words that the doctors had used when my father was dying. It was the last description of his life that I remembered hearing, and it filled me with dread. Non-responsive to me meant the end. Non-responsive meant that my husband lay in a hospital room miles from where I was, and every moment that I watched pass by on the green lights of the clock on the dashboard meant another moment to be with him on this earth that was taken away from me.

When Teresa came out she took one look at the state I was in and offered to drive. On a slow day Teresa can arrive at any destination in the same amount of time as it would take a professional race car driver, so we switched places. As I ran around the car and jumped into the passenger seat I saw she was struggling to move the seat forward so that her feet could more easily reach the pedals.

I sat in my seat for as long as I could, barking out the instructions on how to move the seat.

For a moment I felt like I was still asleep, stuck in a bad dream—one where I knew that someone I loved was in terrible danger and needed me and no matter how hard I tried to reach them, obstacles kept getting in my way.

Finally I could take it no more.

"I'll drive," I told her and hopped back out of the car. We switched places once again, and then I threw the car into gear and we took off for the hospital. It was a quiet ride, and I got us there as fast as I could.

When we arrived, we parked the car and ran towards the hospital doors. I could still hear the nurse's description of Johnny as "non-responsive" ringing in my ears. In the late evenings the doors at Mary Washington Hospital were locked for security reasons. When we made it to the front doors they were closed and the locks were turned on, and Teresa and I began pounding on them, begging to be let in. Once again I was plunged back into the nightmare of obstacles standing in the way of my getting to Johnny's side.

The guards unlocked the door and Teresa and I barreled inside. We ran to the elevator and then up to the third floor, where Johnny's nurse was waiting for us. She took us to see Dr. Berlad and he did not have good news. The hospital had already done a CAT scan of Johnny's head so that they could better see exactly what it was they were dealing with. It appeared that Dr. Berlad's instincts were correct. A blood vessel had burst. Swelling from the surgery had weakened a blood vessel until it had finally ruptured.

"If we go ahead with surgery, there is less than a five-percent chance that he will come out of it alive. If he does survive there is a strong likelihood that he will never wake up," Dr. Berlad told us grimly. "If we do nothing he will likely only live a few more hours."

In the space of a heartbeat Teresa and I both directed him, "Do the surgery. Do whatever you can to save him."

As Johnny was taken into surgery one of the nurses approached us. "You should get whatever family you can to come now," she said, a gentle reminder of how small the odds were in Johnny's favor.

Teresa and I were able to get a hold of Matt and Ross almost right away. They lived in Richmond, about an hour away, so Ross and his wife, Aimee, and Matt were there quite quickly. Next on our list was Johnny and Teresa's older brother, Tommy, who was on a business trip in Atlanta. Teresa tried his phone a few times with little success and soon put that task on the back burner so she could begin coordinating the arrangements to bring Johnny's father, Harding, and stepmother, Melba, up from Mississippi.

It was still early morning and when she couldn't get Tommy on the line Teresa began to make other arrangements for her father and Melba to arrive. It was not as simple as calling them and telling them which flight to catch. Harding was eighty-five years old and some years earlier had suffered a stroke that could at times leave him disoriented. Additionally, he had not yet been told that Johnny had undergone the first brain surgery to biopsy the tumors. We'd thought that once we had a better handle on what sort of fight Johnny had ahead of him we could let Harding know exactly what was happening. In that one evening, all the carefully thought out plans about sparing Harding the pain of knowing what his son was going through ended.

To make things even more precarious, Melba, at age eighty, suffered from the early stages of Alzheimer's. Together their ages and conditions made travel very difficult. We all were acutely aware that the last time Harding and Melba had been on a plane, they had been overwhelmed by the process and the people, and for a time, had lost each other in the airport. It was not an experience we could put them through alone again.

Luckily Teresa did have someone in Mississippi who she knew she could count on for help, even at close to two o'clock in the morning. After returning from their religious retreat, Teresa's friend, Kathy, had been well aware that Johnny was very ill, and so it was Kathy that Teresa called that evening to help get Harding and Melba to Virginia.

When Teresa called her friend at a little after two in the morning and asked Kathy to purchase three plane tickets from Mississippi to Baltimore, and then escort her father and Melba to the hospital, there was not so much as a moment's hesitation on the other end of the phone line. We later learned that Kathy had taken time on the weekend retreat to pray to God to help her not miss any opportunities to serve Him. When the phone rang in the middle of the night only a few days later, she knew it was God answering her prayers and giving her just that opportunity.

As Kathy sprang into action to drive the hour from her house to Brandon, Mississippi, Teresa coordinated with her father's next door neighbors. Calling her father to tell him that Johnny was close to death was not something that she wanted to do knowing that he and Melba were alone. The neighbors agreed to walk over to the house at 6:00 a.m., and when they arrived, Teresa called to speak with her father. After she'd broken the news, the neighbors helped them pack their clothes and medicines. At this point the outlook for Johnny surviving the night was not very positive, and Teresa had the daunting task of trying to explain to her father that he should bring funeral clothes along. By the time Kathy arrived they were ready to go.

Finally, Teresa had been able to get a hold of Tommy on his business trip in Atlanta. It was still very early in the morning and he was able to arrange to take a flight up to Baltimore that would land about an hour before the rest of the family got there. All Kathy would have to do was get Harding and Melba to Baltimore, where the three of them would meet up with Tommy and make the drive down to Fredericksburg in one car.

Johnny and Tommy as youngsters.

Johnny at a meeting.

Johnny graduated from high school in 1966.

Johnny in the National Guard.

A work photo from 2001.

Being home after rehab, Johnny had many good days. He walked one to two miles each day to build his strength.

He had a new appreciation for the world around him.

Johnny when he went deep-sea fishing.

Pictures of a few of the things he made.

Four generations of Walters.

Johnny and me a couple of years after we got married.

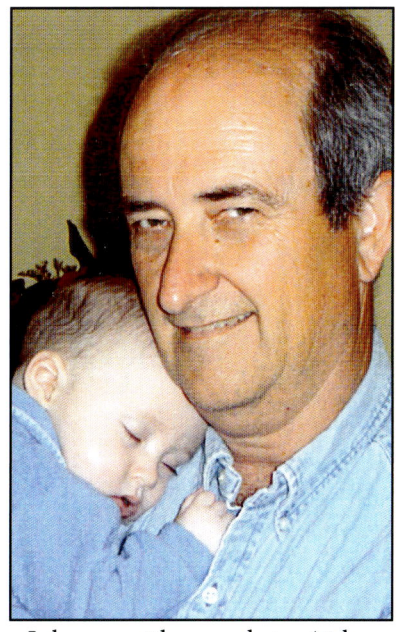

Johnny with grandson Aidan.

Johnny with his father and brother, Tommy.

Johnny with his father and sister, Teresa.

Johnny with sons Mathew (left) and Ross.

Jesus said to her, "I am the resurrection and the life. He who believes in me will live, even though he dies; and whoever lives and believes in me will never die. Do you believe this?
—John 11:25, New International Version

CHAPTER SIX

While Johnny was in surgery, the nurses in the intensive care unit let us use the telephones at their station to organize our family. Their kindness was a double-edged sword. We knew that they were doing more than they needed to do to help us, and for that we were so very grateful. However, at the same time we knew that they were extending us this kindness because they saw that the clock was running down on Johnny's life.

I was so grateful to have Teresa with me that night. The coordination required to get everyone to Virginia was a long and involved task. There were moments when I watched in wonder as her fluid thinking put together the jigsaw puzzle of family pieces in order to get everyone to the hospital.

In between those bursts of activity on the phone as we looked for flights and broke the news to everyone, there was not much else to do except pray. Teresa and I prayed together and we prayed by ourselves. There was a great deal of time where the only thing I could do was sit in the waiting room and do just that—wait.

As night turned to early morning the waiting room began to fill with more and more people. Matt and Ross had already arrived and they were waiting as well. Conversations were going on all around me as doctors and patients and families spoke, sometimes in hushed voices and sometimes in loud bursts that reverberated off the walls. By this time my brother, neighbors and friends were there. Dr. Mussey also stopped by several times throughout the ordeal. But all of it was like so much garbled noise around me.

The people who could help Johnny were with him in the operating room, actively engaged in trying to save his life. As they worked through the night and into the morning all I could do was to have faith in them and faith in God. Even more difficult, I needed to find a source of faith in myself. There were so many times when I thought that I couldn't handle any more. In those moments, there were times that a feeling of helplessness began to creep in and take over my sense of purpose. And at those times when it felt like there was nothing I could do to help, Johnny's voice was steady in my mind and steadied my heart: "I need you to be strong for me."

Turning my mental focus on Johnny and praying to God became like a steady, comforting white noise that surrounded me and kept all the other activity at bay. It was the one contribution that I could make to the events that were underway, and it was the one thing that let me feel as though my husband and I were still connected.

Indeed, faith was a force that connected a great many people that day. The prayer lists that Teresa and Kathy had placed Johnny's name on meant that there were people we had never met before, and likely never would, asking God to give Johnny the strength to fight.

And then there were the prayers that could be found all around us in actions other than the bowing of heads and folding of hands. There was prayer in the kindness of the nurses helping us reach our family that evening. For how better to bear witness to the glory of God than in the kindness of one person to another? There was prayer in the actions of the doctors working tirelessly around the operating table that night. For how better to behold the will of God than by being the vessel through which he works to save a life? And there was prayer in the love of our family and friends, racing through the night to bring us strength and comfort. For how better to see the grace of God than in the eyes of those you love?

During the time that Teresa and Kathy spoke, while planning the flights and coordinating the travel, they paused to pray together. Teresa explained to Kathy how very close Johnny was to death. When the doctor said that there was less than a five-percent chance for Johnny to make it through the surgery alive, none of us wanted to acknowledge that what he was really saying was the certainty was ninety-five percent that Johnny would die that evening. Even survival meant, at best, that Johnny would likely never regain consciousness.

Although we held on to every shred of hope in the doctor's abilities and had every bit of faith in Johnny's fighting strength, the reality of what was happening was grim. Additionally, we had already been graced by miracles more than once that evening. It had been a miracle that Johnny had felt the blood vessel burst in his head and been able to verbalize the experience to the nurse before falling unconscious. It had been a miracle that the nurse had been in the room and in fact been on the telephone with his doctor when it had happened. And it had been a miracle that Dr. Berlad had known exactly what it was that had occurred and been able to direct the actions of the hospital staff to save Johnny's life. How many miracles could we expect in one evening?

Once Johnny was out of surgery and we had received word that he had survived, the prayers continued. The day passed and although Johnny was no longer in imminent danger he was still unconscious. I sat in his room and held his hand, and one by one, members of the family came in to visit with him and join me in trying to coax him back with words of love and hope.

It had been a long flight for Harding and Melba and we decided that instead of driving the thirty minutes back to the house that night, we would get rooms at a nearby hotel. Knowing that Johnny would be upset if he knew that they didn't leave to get a bit of rest, Harding, Melba, Teresa, Kathy and Tommy decided to go to the hotel and get some sleep. On the way out of the hospital they passed a set of open doors. They had almost reached the elevator when Teresa asked the small group to wait for a moment, and she doubled back and walked through the doors into the small, hospital chapel.

Teresa approached the altar and slid into the front pew. The small room was empty and quiet and she sat down and began to pray. After a few moments Kathy joined her and put her arm around her friend, and they sat together in the silence, each one speaking silently to God in her own way.

While sitting in the chapel Teresa reflected on the events of the day. She was asking God to spare her brother's life. While she sat and thought, and prayed, one particular story from the Gospel of John seemed to spring to Teresa's mind. It was one she found very comforting and it helped give her hope for her brother's life:

Now a man named Lazarus was sick. He was from Bethany, the village of Mary and her sister, Martha. This Mary, whose brother Lazarus now lay sick, was the same one who poured perfume on the Lord and wiped his feet with her hair. So the sisters sent word to Jesus, "Lord, the one you love is sick."

When he heard this, Jesus said, "This sickness will not end in death. No, it is for God's glory so that God's Son may be glorified through it." Jesus loved Martha and her sister and Lazarus. Yet when he heard that Lazarus was sick, he stayed where he was two more days.

Then he said to his disciples, "Let us go back to Judea."

"But Rabbi," they said, "a short while ago the Jews tried to stone you and yet you are going back there?"

Jesus answered, "Are there not twelve hours of daylight? A man who walks by day will not stumble, for he sees by this world's light. It is when he walks by night that he stumbles, for he has no light."

After he had said this, he went on to tell them, "Our friend Lazarus has fallen asleep; but I am going there to wake him up."

His disciples replied, "Lord, if he sleeps he will get better."

Jesus had been speaking of his death, but his disciples thought he meant natural sleep.

So then he told them plainly, "Lazarus is dead, and for your sake I am glad I was not there so that you may believe. But let us go to him."

Then Thomas (called Dydmus) said to the rest of the disciples, "Let us also go, that we may die with him."

On his arrival, Jesus found that Lazarus had already been in the tomb for four days. Bethany was less than two miles from Jerusalem and many Jews had come to Martha and Mary to comfort them in the loss of their brother. When Martha heard that Jesus was coming, she went out to meet him, but Mary stayed at home.

"Lord," Martha said to Jesus, "if you had been here my brother would not have died. But I know that even now God will give you whatever you ask."

Jesus said to her, "Your brother will rise again."

Martha answered, "I know he will rise again in the resurrection at the last day."

Jesus said to her, "I am the resurrection and the life. He who believes in me will live, even though he dies; and whoever lives and believes in me will never die. Do you believe this?"

"Yes Lord," she told him, "I believe that you are the Christ, the Son of God, who was to come into the world."

And after she had said this, she went back and called her sister, Mary, aside. "The Teacher is here," she said, "and is asking for you." When Mary heard this, she got up quickly and went to him. Now Jesus had not yet entered the village but was still at the place where Martha had met him. When the Jews who had been with Mary in the house, comforting her, noticed how quickly she got up and went out, they followed her, supposing she was going to the tomb to mourn there.

When Mary reached the place where Jesus was and saw him, she fell at his feet and said, "Lord if you had been here, my brother would not have died."

When Jesus saw her weeping and the Jews who had come along with her also weeping, he was deeply moved in spirit and troubled. "Where have you laid him?" he asked.

"Come and see, Lord," they replied.

Jesus wept.

Then the Jews said, "See how he loved him!"

But some of them said, "Could not he who opened the eyes of the blind man have kept this man from dying?"

Jesus, once more deeply moved, came to the tomb. It was a cave with a stone laid across the entrance.

"Take away the stone," he said.

"But Lord," said Martha, the sister of the dead man, "by this time there is a bad odor, for he has been there four days."

Then Jesus said, "Did I not tell you that if you believed you would see the glory of God?"

So they took away the stone. Then Jesus looked up and said, "Father I thank you that you have heard me. I knew that you always hear me but I said this for the benefit of the people standing here, that they may believe that you sent me."

When he had said this, Jesus called in a loud voice, "Lazarus, come out!"

The dead man came out, his hands and feet wrapped with strips of linen, and a cloth around his face.

Jesus said to them, "Take off the grave clothes and let him go."

—The Gospel of John, New International Version

As Teresa and Kathy prayed in the hospital chapel, Teresa thought hard about this story and asked God to allow Johnny to have a Lazarus-like experience. With only a five-percent chance of surviving the surgery, Johnny had been as close to death as anyone she had ever known. If he were able to survive the surgery and regain consciousness, she knew it would be a miracle. She also knew that miracles like that occurred for a reason, and she wondered what it was that God would be expecting of Johnny were he to receive a reprieve from death.

Teresa prayed for her father to have more time with his son, and she thanked God for giving the family time to gather around him. Teresa knew her own faith was strong, and she knew that she did not need to see the glory of God in a miracle in order to have a stronger sense of belief. But she also knew that Johnny's faith was not as strong as it had once been. And so she prayed for him to grow well enough to know that he had been saved by God. She prayed that he would heal enough to realize God still loved him and had a purpose for him.

And as the two women sat in the chapel they quietly asked the Lord the same things that Mary and Martha had asked of Jesus for their brother, Lazarus. They prayed for him to come to see that he who believed in God would live, even though he died, and that whoever lived and believed in God would never die.

O Lord my God, I called to you for help and you healed me.

O Lord you brought me up from the grave, you spared me from going down into the pit.
—Psalm 30:2-3, New International Version

CHAPTER SEVEN

At around eight o'clock in the morning the doctor came out to let us know that the surgery was finally over.

"It went really well. He's in the ICU right now."

I went into the ICU and looked at my husband. During his first surgery to remove the tumor the incision had been small, and only a tiny bandage had been needed to cover it. In order to reach the place where the blood clot had occurred, this time, the doctors had been forced to remove a large portion of his skull. Besides having most of his head stitched shut, Johnny was completely unconscious and breathing through a ventilator, and it was difficult to imagine that this was the same man who had only hours earlier been telling me that he was raring to get home and get to work on the yard.

I knew it was a miracle that he had made it through the surgery alive, but the road ahead looked much longer and much rougher than it had only twenty-four hours earlier. Instead of focusing on a plan to fight the cancer, Johnny was now laying in a bed, fighting to breathe. For although he had made it through surgery, the next hurdle we faced was to see if he would wake up, and then to see if he could be taken off the ventilator. The doctors had told us that one of the problems that could occur when being placed on a ventilator was the danger of not being able to breathe on their own afterwards.

As Johnny lay unconscious after the second surgery, only two people were allowed in the ICU room at any time. I spent hours sitting next to him, watching him breathe on the ventilator and waiting for him to do something to let me know that deep in his suspended sleep, he was alright. It seemed like forever that I held his hand and waited.

The first time I felt him squeeze my hand it took my breath away.

That one tiny movement was filled with as much meaning as if Johnny had sat up in the bed and looked me in the eye and said, "I love you." Because I knew that was exactly what he was doing. It was what we had agreed on. One squeeze of the hand meant "I love you, I'm alright, I'm still here and I'm fighting" all rolled up into one simple action, and it sent a jolt of electricity through me and gave me more hope than I dared to have.

When Johnny first woke up it was still quite some time before he could breathe on his own without the aid of the respirator. The doctors had warned us that there were no guarantees that the damage from the burst blood vessel wouldn't be extensive. We knew he had survived the surgery, but we would not know what damage there might be to his brain and his functioning until he woke up.

The effects of the blood vessel bursting were similar to the effects that a stroke victim would suffer from. By God's design the brain's ability to heal itself is quite miraculous. But Johnny's recovery astounded even the doctors. His brain had swelled under the pressure of the blood seeping into his skull, and once the burst blood vessel had been fixed the brain had quite literally bounced back into place.

As Johnny started to wake up he did so slowly, but every step towards full consciousness seemed to go smoothly. It took time, but when he finally could breathe on his own and could talk, Johnny was focused and optimistic. Some of the first things that he said were, "What's next?" and "Now what?"

Johnny stayed in the hospital for three weeks. At first he was being fed through a feeding tube. Finally, one day, he pulled the tube out himself and insisted that I help him eat on his own. I knew that he was going to be strong enough to really put up a fight.

The days passed and although his recovery was nothing short of amazing, we still knew that Johnny would need to go to a rehabilitation facility before he would be able to return home. He still had a great deal of work to do on his motor skills, his ability to walk, and his speech.

There were a few facilities that he could go to and we decided that the Sheltering Arms, which was located in Richmond, Virginia, was the best choice for us. Although it wasn't the closest one to our house, The Sheltering Arms Rehabilitation Hospital was only a ten-minute drive from Ross' house, which gave us another nearby family resource. It meant that Ross and I were able to both be daily visitors during his stay.

When Johnny was well enough to leave, Teresa and I drove him to the rehabilitation center and as we arrived, there was staff waiting to help us inside and get him settled. Having Johnny at Sheltering Arms meant that I would wake up in the mornings and drive seventy-five minutes to get there. I would stay for the day and then drive home in the evenings.

Hospitals and rehabilitation centers have very different functions. The main goal for patients in the hospital is allowing the body to heal from whatever trauma it has just been through. While he was in the hospital, Johnny spent a great deal of his time sleeping. His body and his brain needed a great deal of rest, and the doctors explained that sleep was the body's main resource for healing.

When patients arrive at rehabilitation centers, the goal changes from healing to recovering lost abilities. The schedule at the rehabilitation facility was intense. The medical staff expected him to attend multiple physical, occupational and speech therapies throughout each day. It was exhausting for both of us and there were many days when Johnny felt overwhelmed, tired and frustrated, and there were times when he refused to go.

I would arrive each morning at around nine o'clock and would usually find that Johnny had already eaten breakfast. Meals and activities were done in a large room, and there were times when I would arrive and stand in the doorway and spend a few minutes just watching him. When he didn't know I was there I would often see him sitting in his chair, unresponsive and not eating or participating. There were days when I stood there, amazed and grateful that he had survived his surgery and hopeful at how far he had come against overwhelming odds. And then there were mornings when I would stand in the doorway looking in, needing a few more moments to gather my strength in order to step over the threshold of the building and greet him with the positive outlook that was my necessary contribution to his fight.

No matter what I was feeling in those moments before he would see me, the emotion that would grab hold once our eyes met was always the same. His entire face would light up as though a switch inside of him had been turned on, and pride and joy would fill my heart. Knowing that we still had each other was an immediate reminder of how blessed we were, and love is one thing that can send a surge of strength through even the weariest of souls. I would join him at his table and then after a little while we would start with his therapies.

The speech therapists at Sheltering Arms knew that Johnny's favorite hobby was woodworking. When he first began his therapy they used that hobby to help focus him. In the beginning they showed him pictures of things like hammers, screwdrivers, nails and wrenches. It was clear that Johnny needed to recover from the trauma of the burst blood vessel but I was shocked when he wasn't able to identify any of the objects that had once been his most treasured possessions. It took time, and work, and a great deal more healing, but amazingly by the time he left the rehabilitation center Johnny was able to identify them all.

Johnny had always been highly intelligent and quick-thinking. Watching him struggle to command his thoughts was frustrating for me, and I could see that it was physically demanding for him. However, physical therapy was even more brutal. To try to help him learn to walk steadily, the therapists would strap a large, white belt around Johnny's waist. This was so that if, at any point, he was going to fall, the therapists would have something to grab him with. For a boy who had spent most of his childhood running freely through the woods of Mississippi and for the grown man whose simplest pleasures were long walks, fighting to relearn the freedom of movement was a devastating blow, and the white belt was where he directed his frustrations. How Johnny hated that white belt.

There were times when Johnny's intelligence, past woodworking skills, and natural strength and coordination seemed to taunt him from a time when so many things had come so easily to him. It was often easy to forget the blessings of these same skills, which were the very things that were driving his quick recovery. Although it was slow at first, when things finally began to progress, Johnny made remarkable strides. There were times when it was almost easy to forget that there was still a cancerous tumor deep within his brain.

We soon reached the time when the doctors said Johnny was ready to travel during the day to the hospital and undergo radiation treatments, which were the next step in fighting the cancer.

We decided that he would receive the radiation therapy at the University of Virginia. It was truly an amazing facility. Not only was it a hospital with a cancer center but it was also a research center where approximately 200 researchers worked every day to discover new and better ways to fight the disease.

Johnny went to the hospital several times before receiving his first radiation treatment so that the hospital could make a map of his brain. By studying the layout of his skull and brain, they were able to pinpoint the exact location of the tumor and design a special helmet that he would wear during treatment so that they could target exactly where the radiation would hit.

Johnny was home from Sheltering Arms about one month before he was actually ready to begin his radiation treatments, which would be every day, Monday through Friday, for six weeks in Charlottesville, Virginia. When the treatments did start, many of Johnny's friends offered to drive him to his treatments and spend time with him. Tommy and Teresa had also been eager to let us know that they wanted to help in any way they could, so they took turns coming north to stay at our house and drive him down for the daily radiation treatments. At this point, with either Tommy or Teresa visiting, I felt it was a good time to return to work.

Returning to work was my first break away from Johnny's illness since we had first realized he had brain cancer. It was very difficult for me. Although it was Johnny who was sick, we had battled his disease thus far as a team. Since the day Dr. Mussey had given us the news of the tumors and Johnny had asked me to be strong for him, we had not been apart for more than a few hours when I would return home alone in the evenings. I struggled with the fear that I was abandoning him for this course of his fight, but Johnny knew I needed to return to work, and he was so happy for the opportunity to spend time with his brother and sister when they each came up to stay with us.

As hard as it was to return to work, it was also a refuge for me during those few weeks. It was with mixed feelings that I would wake up in the morning and get myself ready to go to the base. There were some mornings when I would go downstairs and prepare a large breakfast, and Johnny and I would sit with Tommy or Teresa at the table and eat and read the paper and talk about the news. These were the days when it seemed as though the weeks prior had been a strange, nightmarish aberration in our lives, and there were moments when I felt almost like none of it had actually happened at all.

My friends and coworkers welcomed me back with open arms and did all they could to make things easy for me. My supervisors made it very clear that they understood that my timetable had become one of day-to-day events. They assured me that I was only to accomplish what I thought I could, and if there was anything I needed, I had only to ask them.

I was extremely lucky. There were days when I would go in and be clear-headed and productive. These were usually the days we had spent having breakfast together in the kitchen. Mornings I had spent in the positive and optimistic outlook of Tommy or Teresa getting ready to help their brother face the fight of the day.

Being able to talk to longtime friends at work about what we were going through was another blessing. Since the moment in the car when Johnny had asked me to be strong from him, I had succeeded in doing just that. I was proud of the fact that I had been able to do that one thing for him, but without those times when I could sit in my office and talk about our ordeal with my coworkers, I'm not sure I could have kept up that strength for much longer.

For my Father's will is that everyone who looks to the Son and believes in him shall have eternal life, and I will raise him up at the last day.
—John 5:40, New International Version

CHAPTER EIGHT

As it is with many people, prayer was introduced into Johnny's life at a young age. He prayed with his family many times throughout the day when he was a child—at meal times, before bed, in church and on special occasions. I too remember learning about prayer when I was young. The Lord's Prayer, bedtime prayers, prayer after communion, and of course whispered prayers to God for all of the things a small child wants.

And then, at some point, prayer left our lives.

I'm sure there were times over the years when we found occasions to pray, but for the most part we lived day to day without thanking God for the things that we had, or for asking him for the things that we needed. We thought we were lucky. In a way it was arrogance. We thought we were successfully providing for ourselves everything that we could ever need. Family, home, career, everything we had—and we had so much—felt hard-earned and hard-won. And, like many people who work hard and achieve a certain level of success, we thought we were completely self-sufficient.

And then Johnny became sick and as quickly as it had left our daily routine, prayer came rushing back into our lives.

There had been two long days in between the appointment for the MRI and the follow-up with the neurologist who had given us the results. For the most part we had soldiered on during those two days, trying our best to have a positive outlook, and to maintain a sense of normalcy. But with so much of the unknown looming ahead of us, those days had felt like years, and the bleakest times I had ever experienced. And during many of those moments of waiting we had been silently praying. It had been almost an immediate, instinctual, unconscious reaction, this need to start a dialogue with God. And after going without this sort of communication for so long, in the beginning they had been private conversations, each of us offering up our own quiet pleas for help and good news.

Without a voice answering us back, it is easy at times to feel as though prayers are just a one-sided conversation. It seems as though many people who pray to God in times of crisis maintain a glimmer of hope that just this once, in their direst moments of need, perhaps the heavens will open and a reassuring voice will speak back to tell them that everything will be alright. Thus far, I don't believe it has ever happened this way. Likewise for Johnny and me, God chose another way to answer our prayers. He chose another way to give us strength. He chose to answer us through the voices of others.

If there is any doubt as to where the twists and turns in our life lead us—the path God has chosen for us to walk—I find that doubt assuaged by the people God chooses to cross our paths. Almost immediately after Johnny's diagnosis, he had called his sister, Teresa, to let her know the news. Teresa had been on a spiritual retreat that week and had told those with her that we were awaiting news about her brother's diagnosis. And those people who she had told had begun to pray for him. And they had placed his name on prayer lists within their own congregations, and others had soon come to pray for him as well. Like a pebble tossed into a lake, the ripples of prayer had reached out in waves until numbers far greater than we could ever have imagined were offering their silent strength to us through those words they spoke to God.

The enormity of this is easily overlooked. But when I stop and think about it I can see the handiwork of God in this prayer chain. In the idea that miles away from us, in cities and towns we had never visited, people whom we had never met, people whose lives we had never touched, were in their private conversations with God, asking Him to give us strength and guidance.

We had received so many prayers from so many places. There had been the couple who ran the dry cleaners that we frequented, and who went to church on a daily basis, including Johnny in their prayers. There had been the people whom Johnny and I worked with, who had quietly prayed for us and who had quietly inquired as to the strength of our faith in God. From the prayer chain that had been started by Teresa's friend, Kathy, we had received letters and emails from all over the south, wishing us well and informing us that we were in people's thoughts.

Knowing these prayers were being said for Johnny had been one of the first ways that he and I had begun to think about God's place in our life, and they had been, perhaps, the first little nudge we had received from God, guiding us back to our faith.

As we dealt with the illness, and the treatments, and the recoveries from the occasional setbacks, we found comfort in the ways in which God had become present in our lives once again. Although I had broached the topic of joining a church with Johnny many times over the years of our marriage, we finally began to search in earnest for the right community. Our search brought us to Reverend Ed Johnson of Dahlgren United Methodist Church. It is a medium-sized congregation located in our town and we were welcomed with open arms into the fold by Reverend Johnson and the church members.

Reverend Johnson not only welcomed us into his church but he reached out to Johnny and me, and spoke to us often, trying to help us find a way back to our faith in God. He was available to us in many ways, from taking the time to address the troubling questions of how God can let an illness like cancer strike a soul like Johnny's to simply opening up the sanctuary on the occasional evening to let Johnny and I inside to pray.

These evening visits were a great comfort to both of us. We would pray silently, and with each other aloud. And no matter what kind of day we had, no matter what kind of symptoms of Johnny's we were dealing with, these quiet moments in God's house always worked to soothe us and renew our hope and our energy to get through the days ahead.

When we first began to attend church I remember asking

Johnny about God and his prayers to Him, and what he was asking for. And Johnny always frustrated me so greatly in his refusal to pray for God to make him healthy. He would never pray to God to cure him or make the cancer go away. He didn't feel it was the right thing to ask for. It was, at times, infuriating.

I never had a problem asking for these things. In fact, I would gladly beg, barter and plead with to God to cure Johnny. But whenever I asked him about what he prayed to God for, Johnny always responded by telling me that he was asking for God's will to be done. His only prayers were to ask God to help him understand and accept His plan for him.

Johnny and his friend, Steve, had had many conversations about where he was with everything regarding his illness and his outlook on his fight against it. He had told Steve that he had an overwhelming sense that God was going to take care of him. It had been something he felt he could just have complete faith in, even though he didn't know what it meant.

He had told Steve he was grateful in some ways for the cancer because it forced him focus on many things that were important in life. He had gone on to say how he had realized he had lost focus on important matters such as his spiritual life, and he knew that God knew it would take something like this to get his attention. Johnny's submission to God and His will had been complete.

This was, perhaps, one of the ways in which Johnny was able to trust God more than I was. It is, in fact, proof to me that even though religion had not stayed in the forefront of Johnny's life, his faith had been so deeply embedded that it had never entirely left him.

In fact the strength of Johnny's faith as it returned to him and became something he was consciously aware of had been inspirational to me. It had become quite obvious to me that this unshakeable faith had never fully left him, but perhaps just taken a supporting role in his life and how he lived it. For how many of us in times of great strife, facing a daunting illness and the uncertainty of what will become of their health, can ask of God only for the strength to accept His will?

But somehow, even though I had not had this same sense of faith in the beginning, even though I'd known only how to ask God for what I'd wanted, the Lord had seen fit to grant me a moment of proof as to the power of prayer.

So often in my life I had heard about the power of prayer, but I had never actually believed that it was a power we were capable of physically feeling until I'd experienced it myself. One of the things that Dahlgren United Methodist had done for us was have a special service for Johnny. In the south this service is often referred to as the "laying of the hands." Simply, it is a prayer service focused on bringing the power of God down upon a person for various reasons. It is done, at times, during baptisms, confirmations and ordinations to ask God for a spiritual blessing or gift.

The laying of the hands ceremony has its roots in the Old Testament. It can be found referred to in a few places, including:

> *Is any one of you sick? He should call the elders of the church to pray over him and anoint him with oil in the name of the Lord.*
> —James 5:14

> *They will pick up snakes with their hands; and when they drink deadly poison, it will not hurt them at all; they will place their hands on sick people, and they will get well.*
> —Mark 16:18

It is a deeply symbolic ceremony and one in which most of the congregation had taken part. Johnny and I had stood in front of Reverend Johnson and Johnny had been anointed with oil. Reverend Johnson had then taken his hands and placed them on Johnny and asked for God to work through him, to give us the strength and power that we needed in our time of strife.

There had been so many people from the congregation present, and it had been their participation that had so moved me and allowed me to physically feel this power that I had always heard about. One by one each person in the congregation had placed their hands on the shoulders of those next to them and in front of them. This chain of humanity had reached from the very last person all the way to where Johnny and I had been standing as we had felt the hands of others rest on our shoulders. And together we had prayed. And in this way, interconnected as one single group, the faith of all those people had surged through us, and I could feel electricity in it.

The experience had been overwhelming. I wanted so much to speak, to thank them, but I had been rendered completely silent. Tears streamed down my face in awe of what I had just witnessed and felt.

And in that moment, I had understood what Johnny had been praying for all along. That the faith he'd had to ask God only for the ability to understand and accept His will was something that I could and should be asking for as well. And something that I knew He would grant us when we needed it. And he did.

When I tell people about the hard times that Johnny and I went through, and I speak about the frustrations of helping him get through his day-to-day tasks when he was in his worst health, I know that it was God's strength that helped me through it. When I saw Johnny struggling with things that had always come easy to him, I knew it was God's strength that was allowing him not to give up.

God may not have answered me in a booming voice during those prayers, when I scolded him for being so unfair as to allow Johnny to suffer through his illness. But he whispered to me, through the voices of others, to have faith. God did not part the heavens and reach down to heal Johnny and make everything alright for us. But He did reach out through the hands of others and give me the strength to know that no matter what happened, He would be there for us through it.

In His hand is the life of every creature and the breath of all mankind.
—Job 12:10, New International Version

CHAPTER NINE

From the late summer into the fall, Johnny and I began to return to a somewhat normal life. The side effects of his short-term memory caused us the most difficulties. I guess, in one way, this was because I craved routine in life it was easy for me to create ways to help Johnny get through the day while I was at work.

In addition to preparing his lunch for when I was out of the house, and figuring out a way to be sure all of his medicine was being taken when I was at work, I used a large white board. Every morning I would write the date and information that I wanted to be sure he knew. A typical day might look like this:

> Today is Thursday, September 14, 2007.
> Lunch is roast beef on rye on the top shelf of the refrigerator.
> Today would be a good day to: walk to the mailbox, watch television, or sit outside and read a book.
> Tonight we are going to go see a movie.

One morning, I suddenly had the urge to write another line at the bottom of the board. It said:

> I love you very much. I cannot wait to see you when I get home.

Johnny loved that. He must have told me a hundred times that day how great it was to read that every time he looked at the board. And so it too became a part of my morning ritual.

But in that way, our lives were normal. When people ask about all of the additional things we had to do to compensate for his memory loss and the coordination problems he had stemming from trouble on the right side of his body, they always seem to anticipate hearing about the difficulty in making adjustments. Often times, I hear, "Oh, that must have been so hard to remember to do every day," or, "It must have been a terrible blow to Johnny to have to rely on you so much." But even now, having gone back and dissected every single moment of that time to retell this story, none of it was difficult.

When Johnny had first came home from Sheltering Arms, he couldn't tie his tennis shoes or button his shirts straight. It had all been a part of the damage inflicted upon his coordination, and so in the mornings, for some time, I would help him get dressed. But for Johnny, instead of it being an upsetting experience, it had just been something he'd tacked on to the end of the list of things he'd had to practice and relearn to do. And he'd never given up trying to make it work.

There were days when, if he'd concentrated and taken his time, he could button a shirt perfectly, and when he did he was proud of the accomplishment. His ability to turn setbacks into challenges had been a vital part of getting him to focus on getting better. As for the shirts, there had been a comedian who had done an act about his wife treating him like a child and picking out his clothes every day because she didn't like what he chose to wear himself. Johnny used to laugh and say that was what was really going on when I helped him dress in the mornings.

The fact that we were still so aware of how much we meant to each other, and our ability for Johnny to rely on me just as much as I relied upon his optimism and good humor, had made me believe with all of my heart that everything would turn out alright.

As with all things in life, at times our ability to laugh at the bleakest things is what gives us the strength to move on. One of the things that happened that fall unfolded like a scene out of a comedy routine, and was one of the times when I know we were both blessed to be able to step back and see the humor in things as they occurred.

Johnny had always enjoyed every aspect of food, both cooking it and eating it. And as much as he had enjoyed a home-cooked meal all through our marriage, if there had been a reason to go out to a restaurant, Johnny would find it. For some reason, when he'd returned home after rehab, his need to go out had increased. Part of me suspects it was because, for much of the day he would be cooped up at home, and part of me knows that he enjoyed us sitting someplace together at the end of the day, talking about any subject in the world and enjoying good food just like any other couple.

One evening we went out to a restaurant and were seated at a table. We ordered our drinks and then Johnny got up to use the rest room. I sat quietly, probably after what was a long day at work, and didn't think about much in particular. My mind wandered and it was a few minutes before I realized that it was getting to be unusually long for him to be away.

Because I hadn't been paying attention to the time, I wasn't sure if it had been five minutes or ten that had passed, and so I wasn't particularly nervous or panicked, just concerned. I stood up and walked towards the back of the restaurant, where the restrooms were. And lo and behold, who did I pass on my way there? Johnny. Sitting at a table, eating nachos and drinking a Coke, which he had ordered from the waitress (who no doubt thought he had a twin, or that he had ditched me to dine alone after a marital argument of some sort).

I stood there and asked him, "What are you doing?"

He looked surprised to see me. His short-term memory had made him get to the bathroom, and then come out to the restaurant and forget who he was with or why he was there. So he simply sat at a table, ordered his nachos and waited to see what would happen next. I sat down at the table with him and as frustrating or embarrassing as many people think the experience might have been, we both burst into laughter.

I am not sure if many people would have that reaction in his place. I am not sure if I would. But for Johnny, because there were leaps forward in his progress mixed in with setbacks or mishaps like this one, he took it all in stride.

One leap forward during this time was a trip that we took to Mississippi, to visit Johnny's family. We weren't sure how the travel and the trip would affect Johnny—if he would tire out or have a difficult time—so we embarked with some trepidation. In retrospect it was probably one of the things that we did in the quest to return to a more normal time, when travel had been something we'd done so often. Everything went without a hitch. We flew into Mississippi and had a wonderful visit with everyone.

When we returned home, Johnny was relaxed and confident. We started to feel as though we might even be able to plan another vacation to enjoy soon. And then we found out that the cancer had come back again.

The tumor that had been surgically removed was growing back. It was a harsh blow, but Johnny had been home and life had just begun to feel normal again. We weren't ready to let the news of the tumor chase those feelings away. We felt strong and optimistic. The trip to visit his family only weeks before had served to lift his spirits greatly and we had settled into a comfortable existence that allowed us to dare to plan the trips we might take in the future. We talked about the future, and neither of us doubted that it wouldn't be long before all would be completely back to normal again.

The initial discovery that this disease has entered your life is a devastating blow. So it is odd that upon receiving the news that one of the tumors had reappeared, Johnny and I were shaken but upbeat. We knew it was a possibility. Anyone who has had any form of cancer is always aware of the chances, odds and likelihood of it returning, but we had been through so much, and Johnny had fought every setback so valiantly, that we remained optimistic.

When we looked at our options there was nothing that made us feel as though this battle wouldn't be won as well. Of the two tumors that Johnny had originally been diagnosed with, the one that had returned was the one that had been close to the surface. Although the surgery had resulted in the trauma of the burst blood vessel, the tumor itself had been in a location that lent itself to being eradicated. Much more difficult had been the tumor lying deep within his brain, and radiation had rid that one completely from his body. That fact alone gave us all the hope we needed that this tumor, too, would soon leave for good.

We had big decisions to make and although our hope did not waver, Johnny was not sure at all what he should do. The surgery to remove a tumor had been traumatizing enough the first time around. Although a burst blood vessel (as had happened the first time) was still something the doctors said was a rarity, there were other dangers that we had to consider. Because of the location of the tumor, a hairline difference in how they removed it could mean paralysis. Radiation was no longer an option as Johnny had too recently been through that as well. His bone marrow had stopped producing red blood cells and because of this we would have to wait until their numbers came back before we could consider going that route again.

Lucky to be in a country with such advanced and intense cancer research programs, Johnny and I were even luckier to live in an area that put us close to the Duke University Comprehensive Cancer Center. And further, the cancer center at Duke was the home of the Preston Robert Tisch Brain Tumor Center. Well-known for taking aggressive actions on patients afflicted with brain tumors, Duke was where we headed immediately to find out about securing Johnny a place on a clinical trial.

I remember my initial reaction to the Duke center. The hallway was covered with pictures of survivors who had received their treatments at Duke. Their letters of thanks and updates on the wonderful and inspiring outcomes of their lives were just overwhelming. The staff there took Johnny's picture and I knew that one day it would be hung on the walls and we too would have a chance to write in about the wonderful life we were having.

Somehow, in the midst of the medical testing and the decision to go to Duke, Christmas came and went with unexpected feelings. We enjoyed the holidays and in light of the past year, they inspired a feeling of great thanks and love. We were also fortunate to enter the holidays feeling as though the treatment Johnny would soon be receiving had a good chance of eradicating the cancer again.

His treatment began on December 30, and the first program Johnny was placed in allowed him to be out of the medical center, and so we stayed at a hotel near the university, and a nurse was dispatched to give him his daily doses and track his progress. Undergoing these treatments required a great deal of follow-up because at Duke, the aggressive stance against cancer required that as short as four weeks after a treatment was started, the doctors may decide to change to another tack if a great enough success was not immediately seen.

Johnny's doctors were not satisfied with the course he was originally placed on, and the team working on his case decided that further action needed to be taken. We were lucky once again because the clinical trial they placed him on was one that a doctor affiliated with Duke, and located in Fredericksburg, could give him, and track his progress along with those doctors at the Cancer Center.

With this we packed our bags and headed home. The new trial involved a chemotherapy drug that targeted the brain. We were hopeful for strong results, and that hope was what saw us through the difficult times as Johnny's body reacted to the awful things that it was put through.

There were days when it was so difficult to watch what he was going through. I cannot imagine how difficult it is to deal with your body's betrayal on a daily basis, from the ongoing frustrations of short-term memory loss to the terrible physical reactions that Johnny had to deal with associated with the chemo.

The helplessness I sometimes felt, being powerless to make it all go away, were some of the bleakest moments of my life. But odd as this may seem, the bleak moments were still overshadowed by the simple joy of being together and knowing that every moment of agony was payment for the moments of happiness we would have in the future.

Just as sure as I was that everything would work out fine in the end, Johnny too had a sense of certainty about him. He took everything in stride and showed such strength, and I was soon to learn that much of that strength emanated from a complete embrace of his faith in God.

Though I walk in the midst of trouble, you preserve my life; you stretch out your hand against the anger of my foes, with your right hand you save me.
—Psalm 138:7, New International Version

CHAPTER TEN

In the course of this year of reflecting, I read many different things and had many conversations with various people about the stages of grief. People kindly advised me of all the various emotions I would travel through in dealing with the death of a loved one. And as the months went by I began to wonder if I was going to go through any of them at all. For to me, grief seems to be just an overwhelming and all-encompassing emotion. Grief hasn't visited me broken down into neat stages. I wish it had, as that sounds like such a much more pleasant and orderly way to go through all of this. I have only spent the past year swinging wildly between sorrow and numbness, a ride that seemingly has no end.

One of the few things that has given me a sense of focus and a sense of purpose has been working on Johnny's story. It has been as orderly a way as I could manage to deal with grief. But as I have worked on this story throughout the year, there have been so many times that I've felt a rising panic about what I would do when I reached this section. For whenever I have tried to focus on the final weeks of Johnny's life, the details escape me. I'm sure it is a mechanism of defense, being unable to recall the day-to-day minutiae in the time of our lives that marked the beginning of the end of his life. It seems to all have happened in a blur of specifics that I can only distantly recall, even as the end unfolded over an entire season.

So often since Johnny's death, friends and neighbors, people at work, at church, have remarked that I have been so strong. They have commented that I seem to be doing so well and remark in wonder that I have been moving forward, going to work, and working on this story in such positive ways. It makes me cringe a little bit to hear that. For deep down inside, I feel only as if I am a mess.

But then again, there is nobody around to see me on the mornings when I lay paralyzed in bed, not wanting to get up into a world that doesn't include Johnny. Nobody knows that even as I have felt my faith in God renewed by the experiences I have told you about, I have simultaneously questioned the emptiness of the life I feel is laid out before me in Johnny's absence. Nobody has been inside my mind, knowing that it has blocked out many of the details that surrounded Johnny's last days and his death. Nobody knows the emptiness and guilt that I felt on those days when I could not remember even the small moments of joy, which should be so valuable to me that my memory would never let them go.

I may not have had the neat, orderly grieving process that I have read about in books, but thankfully God seems to have had a plan for me. For how much of the time it has taken to write this story has been designed by God to help me heal? I would venture to say all of it. God does not give us more than we can handle, and in the same way, God gives us what we can handle when He knows that we are ready. And so, as my memory seems to come rushing back to me with the change of seasons, I believe that God knows I am ready to remember and grieve the end.

As I write this, it is once again April. For some reason, I have arrived at this point of writing the story on almost the same date that Johnny's health began to take a final turn for the worse. And as I think about it, I am surprised that suddenly, the details that eluded me when I thought about them all year long suddenly seem to be within my grasp.

When I rise in the morning and head into work, the whole world seems to be repeating the same cycle that it was going through as the final events in Johnny's life unfolded.

Nature's preparation for the spring season that begins this month means that rain comes to Virginia. It means that the weather alternately warms and cools wildly, often with no rhyme or reason.

It means that even though some days bring cold and rain enough to require a sweater on your shoulders and a soup bowl at dinner, the days themselves grow slowly longer and lighter.

This mix that happens as the world prepares to burst forth new life for a new year also brings with it a charged volatility. Perhaps it is this feeling that has jolted my memory. This feeling of instability that matches my memory of the emotions that flooded through me as I realized that after a winter of hibernating, something was once more stalking Johnny's health.

It was the beginning of April when he had trouble standing and we decided to go to the emergency room. Johnny was able to walk into the hospital by himself, and we told the doctors of his weakened state. But they had a difficult time figuring out what was wrong. When it was clear that he was sick and that the doctors were going to need time to figure out what the problem was, Johnny was admitted to the hospital.

One would think that being admitted into a hospital, waiting to hear of the ways in which your body was once again betraying you, would make you bitter or angry. But that wasn't Johnny's focus during that time. While he was in the hospital he seemed to find greater importance in the things that he had experienced over the past year, and it was here that we began to talk about some of the miracles he had experienced.

Reverend Johnson notes that Johnny had always felt that there was a chance he would not get better, but felt at peace through his faith in God's control of his life. I suppose that these moments in the hospital, as Johnny and I spoke of his renewed relationship with God, are the best examples of that peace that he had come to find.

There had been times during the past year and a half that Johnny had conversed with God. As Johnny had returned to praying more regularly, his conversations with God had become daily rituals. I had grown used to hearing about them, and they were as much of a comfort to me as they were to him. Times that he would spend walking down to the end of the driveway were often times that he took to speak with God, outdoors, in nature, where he felt God's presence all around him. Often when he walked down to the mailbox, he felt as though someone was walking next to him.

The first time God answered Johnny back, he thought he had lost his mind. I remember it well. It is a memory that makes me smile because the mixture of awe and wonder and surprise and worry all etched in Johnny's face is what made the story he told me so believable and so real.

He had been in the shower and when he'd come out of the bathroom he'd said, "Hey, babe, I've got something to tell you." And then he had explained, "I was praying while I was drying off and God talked to me."

When I had asked him what God had said, Johnny had told me, "He said don't worry. Cathy is with you and I'm with you."

But as much comfort as Johnny had felt from his conversations with God, it was the feeling of the Lord's hand on his back, stopping him from falling, that had been one of the deepest experience of faith that Johnny had. The day it had happened, that year and a half ago, he had explained to me that God had saved him from falling down the steps, and I had always known that there was more to the story, but Johnny had never gone into it in any great detail. I had never pressed him on the subject because it wasn't a story I liked to listen to. No matter how much time had passed I still could feel my heart skip at the thought of Johnny falling helplessly through the air down the steps.

But now, the story came tumbling out.

At this point Johnny was lying in the hospital bed. I knew that something was wrong, that he was coming down with a bad cold or that he was suffering from something that his immune system might not be able to fight without the help of medicine. But I still never for a moment thought that everything wasn't going to be alright. Johnny was still the same man that I had married. He could still find his sense of humor, he still seemed to be a tower of strength, and whatever physical strengths were now limited in him he more than made up for with mental and emotional strength.

To be perfectly honest, it seemed to both of us like this visit to the hospital was perhaps the result of him trying to do too much too fast, and yet we both assumed that he would be back at home in no time at all.

So, when he lay in bed and held his hand out into the air and started to cry, I have to admit that I was momentarily surprised.

"What's wrong?" I asked him gently, reaching out to hold his hand.

The tears made his eyes shine and he looked both proud and amazed as he said, "I'm so proud God touched this hand."

I looked at his hand and at him, and asked, "When?"

"The day I fell down the steps."

Johnny had never gone into great detail about that day.

"Jesus was a carpenter," Johnny said. "And he came to see me and he held my hand and he talked to me."

"What did he say to you?" I asked.

Johnny didn't seem to hear me. He was quiet and I pressed on with another question. "What did he look like?"

"He had on a long, white robe with red stripes on it, and he reached out and touched my hand," Johnny said.

"Did he say everything was going to be alright?" I asked, getting back to what I really wanted to hear.

After all we had been through in the past year, to be back in the hospital once again, I still needed to hear some reassurance about what the future held for us. I wished that Jesus had come and visited me and talked to me and answered my questions about what lay ahead for Johnny. But he hadn't. So I just wanted to hear Johnny say that Jesus had told him everything would be alright. I had become so used to seeking out second opinions from doctors regarding his illness that it made perfect sense to hope that God too would provide us with a second opinion.

Johnny remained silent and I asked him again.

"Did he say that everything was going to be alright?"

I was starting to feel panicked.

"Maybe God's touch healed you and you're going to be okay?" I prompted.

With a faraway look on his face Johnny nodded his head and gave me a smile, "Maybe."

Peter replied, "Repent and be baptized, every one of you, in the name of Jesus Christ for the forgiveness of your sins. And you will receive the gift of the Holy Spirit. The promise is for you and your children and for all who are far off—for all whom the Lord our God will call.
—Acts 2: 38-39, New International Version

CHAPTER ELEVEN

I have often wondered about Johnny's description of Jesus as he appeared to him that morning in our home. Johnny was quite descriptive about the event, and what stood out to me the most was what our Lord wore when He appeared to him. There is no significance to Jesus appearing in a robe; historically, that was the clothing of the time and place when he lived on earth. However, that the robe would have red stripes was a detail that stood out to me in Johnny's description. Red is not a color often associated with Jesus nor is it one often used in the church for its symbolism, except for one holiday: Pentecost.

> *When the day of Pentecost came, they were all together in one place. Suddenly a sound like the blowing of a violent wind came from heaven and filled the whole house where they were sitting. They saw what seemed to be tongues of fire that separated and came to rest on each of them. All of them were filled with the Holy Spirit and began to speak in other tongues as the Spirit enabled them.*
>
> *Now there were staying in Jerusalem God-fearing Jews from every nation under heaven. When they heard this sound, a crowd came together in bewilderment, because each one heard them speaking in his own language. Utterly amazed, they asked: "Are not all these men who are speaking Galileans? Then how is it that each of us hears them in his own native language? Parthians, Medes and Elamites; residents of Mesopotamia, Judea and Cappadocia, Pontus and Asia, Phrygia and Pamphylia, Egypt and the parts of Libya near Cyrene; visitors from Rome (both Jews and converts to*

Judaism); Cretans and Arabs—we hear them declaring the wonders of God in our own tongues!" Amazed and perplexed, they asked one another, "What does this mean?"

Some, however, made fun of them and said, "They have had too much wine."

Peter Addresses the Crowd
Then Peter stood up with the Eleven, raised his voice and addressed the crowd: "Fellow Jews and all of you who live in Jerusalem, let me explain this to you; listen carefully to what I say. These men are not drunk, as you suppose. It's only nine in the morning! No, this is what was spoken by the prophet Joel:

> "'In the last days, God says,
> I will pour out my Spirit on all people.
> Your sons and daughters will prophesy,
> your young men will see visions,
> your old men will dream dreams.
> Even on my servants, both men and women,
> I will pour out my Spirit in those days,
> and they will prophesy.
> I will show wonders in the heaven above
> and signs on the earth below,
> blood and fire and billows of smoke.
> The sun will be turned to darkness
> and the moon to blood before the coming
> of the great and glorious day of the Lord.
> And everyone who calls
> on the name of the Lord will be saved.'

"Men of Israel, listen to this: Jesus of Nazareth was a man accredited by God to you by miracles, wonders and signs, which God did among you through him, as you yourselves know. This man was handed over to you by God's set purpose and foreknowledge; and you, with the help of wicked men, put him to death by nailing him to the cross. But God raised him from the dead, freeing him from the agony of death, because it was impossible for death to keep its hold on him. David said about him:

> "'I saw the Lord always before me.
> Because he is at my right hand,
> I will not be shaken.
> Therefore my heart is glad and my tongue rejoices;
> my body also will live in hope,
> because you will not abandon me to the grave,
> nor will you let your Holy One see decay.
> You have made known to me the paths of life;
> you will fill me with joy in your presence.'

"Brothers, I can tell you confidently that the patriarch David died and was buried, and his tomb is here to this day. But he was a prophet and knew that God had promised him on oath that he would place one of his descendants on his throne. Seeing what was ahead, he spoke of the resurrection of the Christ, that he was not abandoned to the grave, nor did his body see decay. God has raised this Jesus to life, and we are all witnesses of the fact. Exalted to the right hand of God, he has received from the Father the promised Holy Spirit and has poured out what you now see and hear. For David did not ascend to heaven, and yet he said,

> "'The Lord said to my Lord:
> "Sit at my right hand
> until I make your enemies
> a footstool for your feet."'

"Therefore let all Israel be assured of this: God has made this Jesus, whom you crucified, both Lord and Christ."

> *When the people heard this, they were cut to the heart and said to Peter and the other apostles, "Brothers, what shall we do?"*
>
> *Peter replied, "Repent and be baptized, every one of you, in the name of Jesus Christ for the forgiveness of your sins. And you will receive the gift of the Holy Spirit. The promise is for you and your children and for all who are far off—for all whom the Lord our God will call."*
>
> *With many other words he warned them; and he pleaded with them, "Save yourselves from this corrupt generation." Those who accepted his message were baptized, and about three thousand were added to their number that day.*
>
> —Acts 2:1-41, New International Version

Pentecost was the day when Jesus' disciples felt the Holy Spirit descend upon them, a moment marked by the appearance of tongues of fire and the reason why the church uses red during the celebration of the season. It was a moment of incredible significance as this was the last act of the salvation of mankind given by God, and the moment in which the divine body of Christ was extended to his believers through baptism by fire. What Peter said to those who were witnesses of this miracle was, "Repent and be baptized for your sins." And for Johnny, this message was what he took away from those moments in the presence of the Lord and marked a turning point for him as well.

Johnny's move away from faith during his adult years had stemmed in part from the way he had grown to view the world. Highly intellectual, he had dealt with facts and figures and provable realities on a daily basis as part of his work. While moral lessons he had learned as a child from his parents and his church had stayed with him through adulthood and were evident in the way he treated others, it was the faith in a higher power that had wavered. This crisis of faith is something that many people find themselves grappling with. The faith in God that we have as children is often easily pushed aside as we grow up and are faced with many of the stark realities of the world we live in.

For Johnny, the teachings of Jesus had always been the rules by which he'd lived. He had loved his neighbors as he had loved himself. He had done only unto others as he had hoped others would do unto him. This innate goodness and faith in humanity had never wavered in him. But as an intellectual he had always sought to learn more about the world we live in.

Slowly, as he had grown into adulthood and felt the weight of material responsibilities bearing down on his shoulders, he had begun to focus only on ways to safely, comfortably and lovingly maneuver his family and friends through life. And in this way he had slowly begun to place greater faith in himself and his responsibilities as a man, and less faith in God for what His will was.

"Baptism by fire" is a phrase we often use for those times when we are facing a task with little warning, without the luxury of practice or the certain knowledge in the next step to come. In the same way, cancer was Johnny's baptism by fire. It was the moment in his life when his faith in God was put to the test. He knew the miracle of time that he had been granted from the moment the first cells had taken root in his body was a moment of grace from God.

And this is what made the story Johnny told me that day the great miracle in both our lives. For it was in that moment, when God had reached out and stopped him from tumbling, that Johnny had realized the will of God was more powerful than his own. Johnny had known then that it had been God's will that he not die the night the blood vessel burst in his brain. It had been God's will to save him once again as he had tumbled down the steps.

Johnny and I had spent so many hours praying over the past year, and attending church services and looking inward at our lives and our faith. But it had been in the moments that Johnny had spent in the presence of Jesus that he had realized God's plan, and his gift of time had been to guide him back to his faith. And with the knowledge of these miracles, he had also been able to find this faith deep inside him and come to understand that God's will had also been at work when the cancer had formed inside of him. And each and every one of these things were a part of God's greater plan for Johnny, and Johnny's realization of this was what saw him through until the end.

For a while, I did not know how to find the best words that would aptly describe the transformation of faith that took place in Johnny. The ability to come to peace with what he was going through and with whatever the outcome was going to be is a hard thing for me to verbalize with the eloquence it deserves and for many to imagine.

Luckily, I was guided to the below verse from Romans Chapter Five, which I believe comes the closest to describing the way that Johnny's faith blossomed throughout the course of his illness.

> *Therefore, since we have been justified through faith, we have peace with God through our Lord Jesus Christ, through whom we have gained access by faith into this grace in which we now stand. And we rejoice in the hope of the glory of God. Not only so, but we also rejoice in our sufferings, because we know that suffering produces perseverance; perseverance, character; and character, hope. And hope does not disappoint us, because God has poured out his love into our hearts by the Holy Spirit whom he has given us.*
> —Romans 5:1-5, New International Version

God is our refuge and strength, an ever-present help in trouble. Therefore we will not fear, though the earth give way and the mountains fall into the heart of the sea.

—Psalm 46:1-2, New International Version

CHAPTER TWELVE

Eventually Johnny grew very weak. Our visits to the hospital increased, and at one of our lowest points he had to be checked into a nursing home. But the cancer, it seemed, was no longer the issue we were fighting.

With his weakened immune system, and his visits to the hospital and the nursing home, Johnny had somehow along the way been stricken with shingles. He had sores on his head, and there were times when he was so weak it seemed that the illness was taking a harsher toll on him than the chemo ever had. Eventually, the infection seemed to settle into his body, and the hospital sent him home and we were assisted by a home healthcare worker.

We had a bed for him placed in the living room on the first floor of the house, and whenever I felt any shadow of doubt about what lay ahead I had only to think of how hard he worked and how successful he was at getting through all of the physical and mental rehabilitation he had required after the burst blood vessel, and I felt my faith in his ability to battle back restored.

As Johnny's condition deteriorated he spoke less and less. For a man who had been so quick to make others laugh, so able to speak on any topic at any time, the silence took some getting used to. Even the silliness, which had been one of the wonderful surprises of Johnny's personality, seemed to have disappeared at this point.

But I never felt as though he wasn't still strong as an individual, and I never felt as though we weren't still strong as a team. And no matter how quiet he would be, there were still those occasions where he would turn to me and say, "I love you." It always amazed me how simple a phrase could be loaded with so many meanings. For saying "I love you" wasn't just a way for Johnny to tell me what he was feeling. It was a way of expressing thanks for the things that I was doing to help him, a way to recall all of the wonderful times we had shared and a way to remind us both of what we had to be thankful for in each other.

When I would respond back, "I love you too," I knew he understood that it meant that my taking care of him was dwarfed by the enormity of the happiness he had given me for so many years, that my certainty that he would get better was absolute, and that I too was thankful for all that we had found in each other.

And then one Friday morning, I sat Johnny upright in the hospital bed and was feeding him breakfast while we watched the *Today Show*. Johnny had been quiet for so long I was almost becoming accustomed to the silence. When he said, "Turn that up so I can hear it," I tried not to show how surprised I really was, and happily turned the television up louder.

The normalcy of that moment propelled me back to other times and made me feel even more certain that everything was going to be alright. My husband, the one whom I had been married to for so many years, was going to get back to his old self. I remember he ate all of his breakfast and I was so happy, I bordered on being giddy.

The next day, just as suddenly as things had seemed to be better, they changed. Johnny couldn't breathe and we called the rescue squad. I remember it took them forever to get to the house. I felt so helpless in those moments, promising Johnny that everything was going to be alright, promising myself that everything was going to be alright, and promising God a litany of things if he would just make everything be alright.

The rescue squad finally arrived and took Johnny to the hospital.

When I arrived at the hospital the doctors were already hard at work. Steve, Ross and Matt all arrived shortly after I did and we sat in the waiting room, quietly waiting for the doctors to come out and tell us what was going on.

Perhaps the deepest regret that I have is the feeling that I squandered those precious minutes that seemed to stretch out forever before the arrival of the rescue squad. I had been so focused on getting Johnny in to see the doctors, so focused on the belief that this was just another emergency that had to be dealt with and survived, that I had no idea how precious that time would be. For in the end, it turned out that it would be the last time I would see Johnny conscious.

I tried so hard to speed up the most important moments that we might have together without even knowing what I was giving up. I wanted to rush the rescue squad to our house, and then once at the hospital I wanted to rush the doctors to come and tell us how things were. But those moments should have been the ones that I just sat and absorbed. Those were the moments that I should have just sat, quietly grateful because he was still alive. But we don't know those things as they are happening, and like so many others, they slipped through my fingers without my even knowing they were gone.

The doctor came into the waiting room with grim news. "He's not going to make it." It was so difficult to comprehend, but I didn't have the luxury of not facing facts. In the end, it wasn't cancer that would end Johnny's life. It was cancer that had weakened him, ravaged him, and that he had fought so mightily against. But in the end, a simple infection that his immune system had been unable to fight off brought us to this place.

Decisions had to be made and the doctor was asking me to make them then. There was no chance that Johnny was going to get better. There was no chance that he was going to regain consciousness. The doctors were clear, concise, straightforward and as empathetic as they could be in such a cut-and-dry situation. "I need to know from you right now. You only have a minute and I'm sorry, but do you want a do not resuscitate order?"

There were no other options. Somehow I made it through those moments. Somehow I managed not to collapse, not to curl up into a little ball and wait to wake up from this awful dream. Fortunately Johnny and I had broached this subject when he'd had his first brain surgery. It was one of the many gifts he had given me, the ability to make this decision not entirely by myself. I told the doctor that Johnny did not want to be resuscitated, and so that was our decision.

"That is very compassionate," I was told and then as the doctor launched into details of the next steps, everything began to feel very far away and distant until they brought me in to see Johnny in the ICU room. At this point Reverend Johnson had made it to the hospital and he joined us and was yet another source of strength sent to get me through those moments.

Reverend Johnson and I sat next to the bed and I placed my head on Johnny's chest and talked to him as Reverend Johnson prayed. I could hear Johnny's heartbeat and it was comforting and reassuring and I knew that just as I could hear it, he could feel that I was there with him. I stayed like that for a while, until a nurse came into the room. She approached quietly and placed her hand on my back. "I'm sorry, he's gone." She said.

I sat up. "I can still hear his heartbeat," I said, sure that she was wrong. That time had not finally run out. But the monitor had flatlined, and the steady noise I continued to hear through his chest was simply the sound of the ventilator still filling his lungs with oxygen.

Reverend Johnson didn't want me to drive home. I remember feeling numb, but assuring him I was fine. But he insisted that I not be alone on the drive, and so his wife, Pam, came in the car with me and he followed until I reached the house, and then the two of them saw me in and then went home. I remember going into the house by myself and going upstairs and getting into bed, feeling lost in a sea of numbness and sure that it would drown me before I woke up the next morning.

Blessed are those who mourn, for they will be comforted.
—Matthew 5:4, New International Version

CHAPTER THIRTEEN

There was something about the process of planning Johnny's funeral that I believe propelled me forward in the hours immediately following his death. On some levels it was a gift. I allowed myself to be consumed by the need to focus completely on putting together a ceremony that would honor Johnny's life and his faith, and give me and his family the ability to say goodbye to him properly. I am not sure that I would have been able to get out of bed or face the world without this task.

On one hand, funerals seem to be too little, too late. All of the things that we say about our loved ones during eulogies and scripture readings are the very things that we should have been saying to them every hour of every day of their lives. I have always known, on some level, that funerals are not at all for those loved ones we have lost, but instead a way for us to focus and deal with our grief. However, it has not been until very recently, as I have felt the beginning of the heavy weight of sorrow and grief lift, that I really understood the importance of this ceremony for those of us left here on earth to live through our remaining days without them.

There were so many details that needed to be taken care of. Details for the viewing, for readings, for timing, rides to and from the church and the ceremony, travel plans for Johnny's family travelling up from Mississippi. I mentioned to Johnny's boss at the consulting firm he had been working at that we would need six pall bearers. I wanted six people who knew and respected Johnny. I believe I could have asked for a hundred. He immediately found six people and of course, Johnny's friend, Steve, was one of them.

So many of the traditions that surround death have been honed and refined throughout civilization, and they serve so many purposes. Viewing services, as difficult as they may seem in theory, offer the opportunity for some of the most comforting thoughts. It is very difficult to look upon a body lying in a casket and not see it for the empty shell that it is. And in that thought there can be such hope and such grace, for that is always the moment that comforts me, giving me the knowledge that the spirit, and the essence that once thrived inside that shell, is no longer here. And with a spirit and soul as vibrant as Johnny's there can be no question that it wasn't a flame that was put out, but one that was set free.

Every time one decision was made, another one appeared and so it was like that, moment by moment, that I made it through to the funeral. And then that day arrived. And with it the realization that the final goodbye had arrived and that we were left here alone without our loved ones. When the morning finally arrived, I pivoted from being propelled forward by my own actions to having to hand the reins over and be propelled forward by the realization of my loss. I did not think I would be able to make it into the church, let alone sit through a service, without breaking down.

I had been able to maintain some level of strength over the past year and a half because Johnny had been the foundation that my strength was built on. Nothing had dampened my belief in him or his ability to beat the odds even as they had stacked up mightily against him. But now, without him there to give me a reason to be strong, I wanted nothing more than to curl up into a ball, close my eyes and never wake up.

But, in the end, Johnny once again provided me with the strength I needed, because deep down I knew that the life he had lived deserved recognition, and it was not an option to walk away from that before the very end.

I managed to pull myself together. It was a lot more difficult that that sentence makes it sound. Approaching the church, I felt sure that my legs would simply give out, or that the actual, physical pain I was feeling from his loss would crush me before I could walk inside and sit down in a pew. I sat between Ross and Matt, and in their father's absence they both gave me strength.

I have been told that there were many people inside the church that day, but truth be told I do not remember. The service was not long at all. Or maybe it was. Much of it was a blur. But then Reverend Johnson spoke about Johnny's life and his accomplishments. He spoke about Johnny's Lazarus-like miracle after the bursting of the blood vessel in his brain. And he spoke about the man who had come back to enter the fold of faith, humbled and strengthened by his faltering health.

As one of the people who had witnessed Johnny's return to his faith in God, Reverend Johnson knew first-hand of Johnny's deep desire to encourage others to turn to God. One verse of scripture that does stand out from that day of sorrow and grief and celebration is:

> *In the time of my favor I heard you, and in the day of salvation I helped you. I tell you, now is the time of God's favor, now is the day of salvation.*
>
> —2 Corinthians 6:2

Reverend Johnson noted that Johnny had expressed thankfulness for what he had been going through, for being given the chance to battle cancer. For not only had he found the strength in himself to not give up, but more importantly he had found the strength in his soul to realize the value of the gift of faith, and the gift of life, and the chance to have so many additional days not to squander any of it. It was a lesson he would have shouted from rooftops had he been able to.

The thought that it had taken an emergency of sorts to wake him up from the hazy existence he had felt he had been living, the thought that it had taken cancer to give him the clarity to recognize the beauty and importance in a faithful life, was something that deeply frustrated him. As a man who had always worked to achieve his goals, he had viewed it as wasted time that he could have spent so much better serving God and others even more than he had.

And, somehow, through the stormy rage of emotions that hovered inside of me, I knew that Johnny was with God. It was a terrible and a bittersweet realization, and I like to think that if it were not for the binding grip of the loneliness that I felt, I would have been able to celebrate the fact that the husband I'd lost was finally at home with God.

After the funeral services ended and we arrived at the cemetery I was given a yellow rose off the casket as we were leaving. I dried it and placed it in a glass jar and still have it in our home today.

The women of our church prepared a great deal of food afterwards. People were invited back to our home after the ceremony and many came. I remember people walking through the house, amazed by all of the wood furnishings and decorations that Johnny had built over the years. These things were tangible evidence of his time here, and beauty that he added to the world.

In those hours, as had happened during the viewing, many people came up to me and told me stories about Johnny. Laughter dotted the house that afternoon as people relived moments of joy that Johnny had brought into their lives. I remember distinctly one man approaching me and talking about the sermon that Reverend Johnson had given, and Johnny's faith. He said to me that he had known that Johnny was a Christian simply by the way he had treated those around him.

I wish that I could have told Johnny then that there was no need to regret not having the time and strength to travel around and tell how important faith was in life. That his desire to shake people out of their hazy existences and realize what was important was not a goal that he had failed to fulfill. Because as this man said, Johnny had been a Christian and a man of faith his entire life, even when he himself had thought that he had lost that faith, simply because of the way he had been with others. Leading by example is perhaps the strongest way to persuade, and Johnny had always treated people exactly the way that scripture teaches us—with the same love, respect and kindness that we would like the world to show us.

By about two o'clock that afternoon the house had finally emptied out. Family was on the way to the airport, beginning their long journeys home, and food had been wrapped up and stored in my refrigerator by all of those people who had been so kind as to prepare it. After a little while longer, Ross and Matt and my brother left as well. The boys had spent a good portion of the afternoon quietly keeping to themselves, walking around the house and yard remembering all of the things they had done as kids together and with their dad.

And everyone's lives continued.

When I was completely alone I lay across the bed and cried. I cycled through emotions that I didn't even know I had. I was angry at everyone who had been at the house and then left. I was furious at them for having the audacity to keep living. I felt alone and empty and completely helpless.

And when those emotions threatened to turn me inside out, I stopped. It was really rather simple. From that moment, and for quite some time after that, it was much easier to live each day without recognizing that Johnny was gone. It was much easier to go to bed at night pretending he was still in the hospital. I had already spent so many evenings alone in the house over the past year and a half that sleeping alone wasn't that difficult. I had been working at chores that Johnny had always done, and living in a very controlled state of being, and there was comfort in returning to that. And for quite some time, that was how I coped.

Love is patient, love is kind. It does not envy, it does not boast, it is not proud. It is not rude, it is not self-seeking, it is not easily angered, it keeps no record of wrongs. Love does not delight in evil but rejoices with the truth. It always protects, always trusts, always hopes, always perseveres.
—1 Corinthians 13:4-7, New International Version

CHAPTER FOURTEEN

Gradually, as I let myself begin to realize that Johnny was gone from me forever on this earth, and I began to let myself grieve, I also felt a need to do something that would allow others to know this remarkable man as I had. As the Lord does work in mysterious ways, it wasn't too long after Johnny's funeral that I began to look for opportunities to do this. And then, one day, out of the blue, the idea for this book came to me, and so began my journey of healing and reflecting and coming to understand the many gifts of joy that God had given to me through Johnny.

In the year that has passed I have had a great deal of time to reflect on the twenty years Johnny and I shared together. One of the most difficult things about losing a person who had such a strong and positive impact on all those whose lives he touched is thinking about the things that he had still hoped to do in his life.

In the twenty years of our marriage we'd had so many happy and wonderful times in the present that there had never been any doubt that the future would hold so much more. Upon reaching his retirement Johnny and I had often spoken about the days ahead, when we would have the freedom and time to enjoy each other's company, spend more time with our friends and the people we loved, and celebrate together all of the milestones that we expected our family to reach.

One of the things that gives me great comfort is knowing that although Johnny left us way too early, he had positively impacted so many people's lives. Working at Dahlgren, I am surrounded all day by the people and places that had been so important to Johnny, and while I thought that it would be difficult, it is actually like having him with me every day.

In fact, there are so many times when I feel his presence. For the past twenty years Johnny and I had shared our home in King George together. Up until his illness I could probably count on my fingers the number of nights we had spent away from each other. One of the most difficult things that I faced in the time following his death was being at home alone in the evenings. While his time in the hospital over the final year of his life had prepared me in some ways to be alone in the evenings, I always knew that he would eventually be coming home. Facing the nights with the knowledge that he would not be returning was a completely different feeling, and at times the realization of this fact seemed overwhelming.

However, to my surprise, it has been Johnny who has still managed to comfort me in these times. There have been evenings when I have found myself laying in bed, trying to go to sleep, and I have felt a presence in the room. One evening in particular I closed my eyes and felt as though there were someone sitting on the edge of the bed. I immediately assumed that our cat, Molly, had jumped up and perched herself on the mattress, but when I opened my eyes, I saw that Molly, in fact, was across the room. Instead of the fear or confusion that I would have expected to feel, I immediately felt a sense of peace, and knew that somehow, in some way—it was Johnny that was close by.

And as the year has progressed I have come to learn that this sort of feeling, that those who have left this earth are still amongst us, is felt by many people. As most grandparents will tell you, grandchildren are the light of their lives, and Aidan, Johnny's grandson, had certainly been that light for Johnny. Aidan had called him "Big Daddy" and I don't remember a time when Johnny's smile had reached so broadly across his face as it did whenever he'd had Aidan in his arms.

One day Aidan was hard at work on a nursery school project. He traced his hand on a piece of paper and turned it into a picture of a Thanksgiving turkey. His teachers then asked the children to place a name on each of the four feathers that his fingertips had designed. The teacher said that each name was supposed to be the name of someone he was thankful for in his life, and whom he hoped to spend more time with. On one of these fingers, he wrote "Big Daddy."

That night, when his mother asked him about his drawing, he explained the presence of his grandpa's name on one of the feathers. He knew that Big Daddy was no longer there, but that he still wanted to spend time with him anyway. And just as I know that there are times when Johnny is present with me, I know that he is present with Aidan as well. And that gives me comfort.

I decided to pursue writing this book about Johnny because throughout his illness he had always looked ahead to the future and what he could do to make the world a better place. As it had been when he had been in good health throughout his life, even in those bleak times of strife Johnny's outlook had continued to be reflected in the words I had so often heard him say: "What's next?" and "What can I do next?"

One of the things that he had wanted so much to accomplish was to tell others of the lessons he had learned in the final years of his life. He had often spoken of putting his experiences down on paper, and had hoped to be able to write a book that would let others know of the many gifts God had taught him in both the good times and the bad. He had hoped to tell others of the lessons he had learned from his experiences, some of which are only learned by living through hardship.

It had been Johnny's belief that if his suffering had allowed him to learn these things, that perhaps he could pass them on to others who would have the benefit of knowing them without learning them through the same circumstances. Or, more importantly, for those who were going through similar circumstances, that he could serve as a guide to those who were trying to find a way back to their faith and all of the strength that it promised to provide. And of these lessons, first and foremost was his desire to impress on others the great comfort he had found in returning to his faith in God.

In the parable of the prodigal son a man has two sons, and one of them chooses to take his inheritance, leave his father's home, and make his way in the world. He goes out and soon finds that he has squandered that which his father gave him, and is left with nothing. Unable to care for himself, he thinks of his father and his father's unending generosity, which extends even to the poorest people who live on his lands.

Knowing that even though he has squandered that which his father gave him, and that he will still be better cared for as a pauper in his father's land than he will anywhere else, the son returns home. The father's other son stays home, and works the land and lives the uneventful life that is expected of him. As the son who has left returns, the brother who remained is chagrined to see their father's reaction.

This son who has lived his life loyally in his father's shadow, doing everything that has been expected of him, is certain that their father will show his disappointment in the mistakes his brother has made. But instead of punishing this prodigal son for leaving and squandering what he had given him, at the sight of his long-lost child the father opens his arms and welcomes him back, celebrating his return and never holding his poor choices against him.

> *The son said to him, "Father, I have sinned against heaven and against you. I am no longer worthy to be called your son."*
>
> *But the father said to his servants, "Quick! Bring the best robe and put it on him. Put a ring on his finger and sandals on his feet. Bring the fattened calf and kill it. Let's have a feast and celebrate.*
>
> *"For this son of mine was dead and is alive again; he was lost and is found."*
>
> —Luke 15: 21-24

During Johnny's last years on earth he had found God to be very much like the forgiving father in the parable of the prodigal son. For like the child in the parable, Johnny had—as so many people do—stepped away from his faith.

One of the things that makes the parable of the prodigal son so powerful is that its lesson of the love and forgiveness of God is applicable on so many levels. People turn away from God for many reasons and to many varying degrees. For Johnny, turning away from God had never been a conscious decision. It had happened slowly over time, as the day-to-day responsibilities of life, work and family had gradually come to be of greater importance than his relationship with God.

It is a situation that so many of us in this world find ourselves in. Providing for those we love can so easily grow beyond what we envision of the basics and become the pursuit of simply "more."

Before Johnny had become ill we had been very proud of all that we had accomplished together. We had worked hard for many years and had felt the need to reward ourselves for this hard work with things we could purchase. We have a beautiful home, we had money to spend on vacations and all of the luxuries that we thought were the things that made our life so wonderful.

But it hadn't been until Johnny's cancer diagnosis that we had come to see that these things were indeed only distractions from what is truly important during the short time that we are here on earth.

On the day that we had learned that Johnny had his brain tumors, we'd left the doctor's office numb and in shock. We had returned to the parking lot overwhelmed by the crisis we were being confronted with and our immediate reaction had been fear. And the car that we'd sat in, which had once been such an extravagant purchase, had provided us no comfort.

But our strength and our love for each other had. And when Johnny had suffered the burst blood vessel and I had received the call summoning me to the hospital for what we thought were his final moments of life, the house I had been sleeping in did not give me the strength to believe that everything would be alright. But the presence of Johnny's sister, Teresa, had. As Johnny had lay on the operating table that evening, as close to death as a person could get, neither of us had drawn our strength from thoughts of the material things we had managed to collect during our lives. Our strength had been drawn from the love and support of the family and friends who had rushed to be by our side during that time of need.

And as the months had passed by and new challenges had arisen, our strength had been drawn from the prayers that we had whispered silently to ourselves and quietly with each other, as we, like the prodigal son, had returned to God our Father in our moment of need. And these things, our love for each other and the love and the presence of family and friends, and the faith that we had found once again, had been gifts that only God could give us. And much like the father welcoming home his long-lost son in the parable of the prodigal son, they had been the ways that God had thrown open his arms to welcome us home and sustain us during our time of need.

Johnny's certainty about the importance of spreading his story and his experience has left its mark on me as well. When he had been in the weakest health during the very last days of his life, Johnny had still recognized that God had saved him from certain death, on the evening the blood vessel had burst in his brain, for a reason. He had believed that the reason for this miracle was that God had seen fit to give him the gift of time, and allowed him the chance to find a way back to his faith. And it had been very much Johnny's renewed strength of faith that had helped me renew my own.

When we lose someone close to us, the rush of feelings can be overwhelming. There have been times over the course of the past year when the flood of emotions has threatened to drown me. Amongst those emotions have been sorrow, anger, joy, pride, desolation, loneliness, hope, fear and wonder. But the most difficult of these has been confusion.

For me, the questions about my own life that have arisen in the face of Johnny's loss have taken on so many forms. For the twenty years of our marriage I had found myself greatly defined by my role as Johnny's partner. Providing a loving home for Johnny and for our family had been my purpose. During the last months of Johnny's life, being an emotional and physical support for him had been my purpose. They had been responsibilities that had defined who I was and which I had accepted happily, grateful for all of the good times that we had shared, and grateful for the chance to show Johnny how much I loved him and how very lucky I had felt every day to have him in my life. But then, in the wake of his loss, I had found myself struggling with confusion over what purpose in my life remained.

And so as I struggled to answer this question, I found my love for Johnny and my renewed faith in God guiding me to an answer. I found my purpose—and it is to bear witness to Johnny's story. To be sure that the message about the power of faith and the love of God that Johnny wanted so much to spread is told to you.

It is a task that has given me the strength and focus to get through each day without him. In some ways it reminds me a bit of the "honey do" lists that I used to give to him on the weekends. Johnny used to look at these long lists of tasks I needed him to accomplish and chuckle as he headed out the door. And it makes me smile to know that he left me with this "honey do" task to do in his absence.

For the story of Johnny's life and his death are a great testament to the grace of God and I can think of no better way to honor my husband and my Lord than by having shared them with you.

It is so difficult to write the final chapter in the story of someone's life but I find that there is one very special memory that I have of Johnny that I would like to leave you with. It is a small, quiet moment that speaks volumes about him and the way he lived and in the way he died. It shows how deeply he appreciated the gift of his life and how profoundly he had come to accept God's plan for him.

It had been only a week before he would die, and Johnny had been through so much. He had been back in the house from the hospital and even though he had been weak from the infection that had been ravaging his system, I had been certain that eventually he would get well. However, Johnny had known that he was very sick.

God had spoken to him and assured him that he would be alright. Though he had never tried to dampen my hopes for his recovery, I realize now that Johnny had completely come to peace with the path God had chosen for him. While I had assumed that the assurance that Johnny had spoken of receiving from God meant that he would get better and we would have a chance to live many more years together, Johnny had known that it meant that the Lord was preparing a place for him in heaven and that this new journey was nothing to fear.

During those days I had often busied myself with trying to make sure that he was comfortable, and not in need of anything I could provide. I had spent many hours just sitting with him in the house, ignoring any chore that didn't directly have to do with making Johnny more comfortable.

It had been during one of these days that he had turned and looked at me and asked, "Cathy, are you happy?"

It had been a surprising question on so many levels, but most of all because I had answered without even pausing to think about all that we were going through.

"Yes, I am."

And then I had looked at him, laying there in the hospital bed in the middle of our living room, knowing he was feeling terrible, and I had taken his hand in mine and asked him back, "Are you?"

He had closed his eyes for a moment and when he had opened them, he had looked at me and squeezed my hand and answered, "Yes. I am. I'm very happy."